VOGUE KNITTING

CAPS & HATS TWO

VOGUE KNITTING

CAPS&HATS TWO

SIXTH&SPRING BOOKS
NEW YORK

SIXTH&SPRING BOOKS
233 Spring Street
New York, New York 10013

Library of Congress Cataloging-in-Publication Data

Caps & hats two / [book editor, Trisha Malcolm].
p. cm. -- (Vogue knitting on the go!)
Vol. 1 has title: Vogue knitting caps & hats. Butterick. c1999
ISBN 1-931543-24-0
1. Knitting--Patterns. 2. Caps (Headgear) 3. Hats. I. Title: Caps and hats
2. II. Malcolm, Trisha, 1960- III. Title: Vogue knitting caps & hats. IV. Series.

TT825 .C16 2003
76.43'20432--dc21 2002030405

Manufactured in China

1 3 5 7 9 10 8 6 4 2

First Edition

TABLE OF CONTENTS

INTRODUCTION

Function and fun with an accent on fashion was the mission when we assembled this unique collection for *Caps & Hats Two.* We varied the mix—there's a little something for everyone—and included versions of today's most popular styles, with a nod to traditional as well.

Caps & Hats Two offers an opportunity to explore new designs and options on a small scale with a minimal investment of time, materials and space. Caps and hats, the ultimate portable projects, fit easily in your bag, enabling you to slip in a row or two just about anywhere your daily travels take you, turning precious lost moments into rewarding accessories. Try your hand at complicated stitch or colorwork patterns, experiment with surface embellishments, play with new combinations of yarn from your own stash or splurge on a few balls of luxury yarn.

This collection leaves no one out in the cold and is suited to all skill levels. You will find a hat for every reason, season and occasion, from a traditional Scandinavian cross-country ski cap to an exotic faux-fur-edged Mongolian cap and a textile-inspired Peruvian hat with earflaps to keep you protected from the elements. The indispensable beanie is reinterpreted into fashionable city headgear, while a stunning snowflake-pattern beret makes a sophisticated statement. And for little ones, try a sassy neon-bright rolled-brim toddler's cap, a snuggly teddy bear hat or a whimsical Scottie dog cap.

So get a "head start" on your fall and holiday gift knitting. Stuff your yarn and needles into your bag and get ready to **KNIT ON THE GO!**

THE BASICS

Fun to knit and wear, hand-knitted hats and caps are more popular today than ever before. Since the actual amount of knitting is approximately that of an oversized swatch, many knitters are drawn to a variety of styles as a quick way to improve their technique. Other knitters prefer to knit the easiest of styles such as the Ribbed Cap on page 34 and shown opposite the Introduction, in different colors to give as gifts or to just keep on knitting. Since most hats require two or less balls of yarn to knit, and are worn year around by men and women alike as an expression of style, they are the perfect on-the-go project for beginner and expert knitters alike.

CAP AND HAT CONSTRUCTION

A multitude of hat styles for all levels of experience are featured on the following pages. Novices will appreciate the simple beauty of fast-knitting styles in chunky yarns, while the more experienced will delight in the projects that feature unique shaping and challenging stitch patterns and color combinations.

The easiest styles are knit with fast crown decreases or simple sewn pleats at the top. Some are worked flat on straight needles with a back seam that is sewn invisibly from the right side. Others are worked in the round with a circular needle, switching to double pointed needles as the stitches decrease and no longer fit comfortably on the circulars. Most of the hats in this book are worked by beginning at the lower band or brim edge and continuing up the sides, ending at the crown center. The most common top finishing is worked after the last row or round when the stitches are still on the needles. After cutting the yarn, simply draw it through the remaining stitches at the top twice, pull up firmly, and fasten off. The Fair Isle Ski Cap shown on page 87 illustrates a cap that is knit completely straight without decreasing and derives the crown fit by drawing all the stitches together at once straight off the knitting needles. This technique works best with the soft and lightweight yarn that is used in this style and would not be suitable with a different type of yarn.

TYPES OF CAPS AND HATS

CAPS

A cap is a snug-fitting hat that fits closely to the head. The finished circumference of these styles will be smaller than your actual head measurement. Caps are also usually worn above or just covering the ears. One style of cap is called a beanie because the fit just covers the crown of the head and doesn't come down to meet the ears.

Many of the cap styles in this book are designed for everyday wear such as the Flower Topped Striped Cap on page 37 or the Tasseled Cap on page 47. They are accented with simple motifs or embellishments such as tassels and pompoms.

Other cap styles are designed for active outdoor wear and extra warmth especially snow and winter sports either with ample fabric such as the Multicolor Top Tied Hat

GAUGE

It is always important to knit a gauge swatch, and it is even more so with hats as they are designed to fit securely. If your gauge is too loose, you could end up with your hat over your eyes, if it's too tight, the hat will perch oddly at the top of your head.

Making a flat gauge swatch for hats knit in the round will allow you to measure gauge over a 4"/10cm span that will lay flat for better reading. However, when a hat includes a complex stitch pattern knit in rounds, a circularly-knit swatch will test the gauge best and the practice will familiarize you with the pattern—cast on as many stitches as required for the hat. The type of needles used—straight or double pointed, wood or metal—will influence gauge, so knit your swatch with the needles you plan to use for the project. Measure gauge as illustrated. Try different needle sizes until your sample measures the required number of stitches and rows. To get fewer stitches to the inch/cm, use larger needles; to get more stitches to the inch/cm, use smaller needles.

Knitting in the round may tighten the gauge, so if you measured the gauge on a flat swatch, take another gauge reading after you begin your hat. When the hat measures at least 2"/5cm, lay it flat and measure over the stitches in the center of the piece, as the side stitches may be distorted. Keep in mind that if you consciously try to loosen your tension to match the flat knit swatch you can prevent having to go up a needle size.

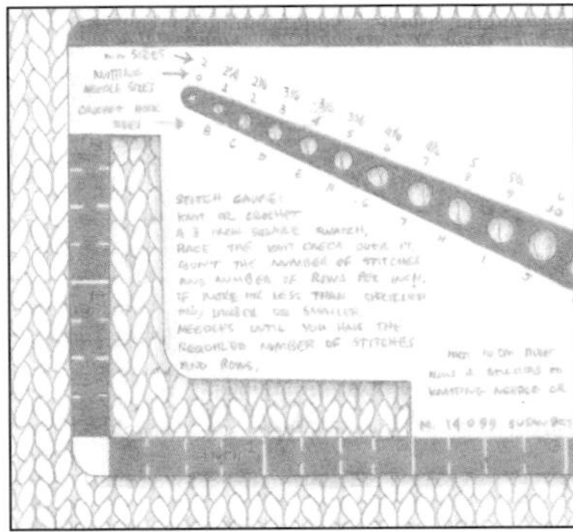

on page 66 or a snug band fit as seen in the Cable Banded Cap on page 63. These simple styles are among the easiest to knit.

Earflap Cap

Many of the styles in this book are the earflap style, which has become a new fashion basic. An organic cable pattern that begins in the earflaps of the Wavy Cable Cap on page 26 is also decreased in a unique crown shaping that ends in a top knot. The Cap with Braided Trim on page 76 has similar earflaps that begin the hat. The Multicolor Earflap Cap on page 50 and Baby's Earflap Caps on page 73 however, have earflaps that are added after completion of the cap knitting if desired. Any of the flaps could be eliminated with some simple advance planning.

Tams and Berets

Tams and berets are flat caps, often topped with a pom-pom or tassels. Since the tam and beret style only has to fit the head around the band edge, the band is usually elastic enough to fit all sizes. When the band is completed, several stitches are increased in one or two rows or rounds. After several inches, decreases are worked at even intervals to form the signature flat shape. Decorative decreases that form the pie-shaped wedges defining the beret crown are a special feature of the style.

The Snowflake Beret shown on page 40 is an elegant example of six wedge shapes that are decreased in the pattern neatly into the crown. Embroidered flowers worked in the same yarn and a braided tassel complete the look.

HATS

Hats are more structured than caps and usually consist of a crown and a brim. Worn since the 10th century, early hats were designed to signify the importance of the wearer. These styles often require more shaping than caps and are both a challenge and fun to knit.

Brimmed Hats

These styles flatter the face and exude an air of sophistication, and they are influenced by traditional millinery techniques. Two of the hats that have been knit with brims are also knit in pieces that are then sewn together as in conventional women's hats.

The Herringbone Cloche on page 22 has three wedge-shaped crown pieces with wrong-side seaming and an increased crown worked outwards. Doubled increases are worked every other row into the herringbone pattern in a unique and invisible way. The Bulky Brimmed Hat on page 54 has five easy pieces that form the crown with outside seams showing along the top for a special effect. Working with needles 1 or 2 sizes smaller than the instructions will result in a tighter gauge and a more standard-fitting style.

SIZING

Most of the hats and caps in this book are sized for women. Those suitable for men and children are indicated in the sizes section of the instructions.

To avoid making a hat that is too tight, measure for head size before you begin to knit. Sizing is particularly important for structured hat styles. To measure, place a tape measure across the forehead and measure around the full circumference of the head. Keep the tape snug for accurate results.

Head sizes used in this book		
SIZE	**INCHES**	**CM**
X-Small	**20**	**51**
Small	**21**	**53**
Medium	**22**	**56**
Large	**23**	**59**

All the hats in the book are given a fit category: very loose-fitting, loose-fitting, standard-fitting, close-fitting and very close-fitting. To change the fit of your hat or cap style, you can experiment with needles sized smaller (for a closer fit) or larger (for a looser fit). Or you may wish to eliminate rows or pattern bands for a style with less depth, or add rows or bands for a deeper hat style.

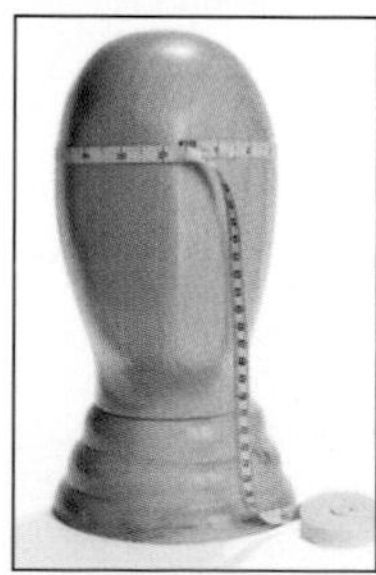

YARN SELECTION

For an exact reproduction of the hats photographed, use the yarn listed in the materials section of the pattern. We've chosen yarns that are readily available in the U.S. and Canada at the time of printing. The Resources list on pages 94 and 95 provides addresses of yarn distributors. Contact them for the name of a retailer in your area.

YARN SUBSTITUTION

You may wish to substitute yarns. Perhaps you view small-scale projects as a chance to incorporate leftovers from your yarn stash, or the yarn specified may not be available in your area. You'll need to knit to the given gauge to obtain the knitted measurements with a substitute yarn (see "Gauge" on page 11). Be sure to consider how the fiber content of the substitute yarn will affect the comfort and the ease of care of your hats.

To facilitate yarn substitution, *Vogue Knitting* grades yarn by the standard stitch gauge obtained in Stockinette stitch. You'll find a grading number in the "Materials" section of the pattern, immediately following the fiber type of the yarn. Look for a substitute yarn that falls into the same category. The suggested gauge on the ball band should be comparable to that on the Yarn Symbols chart (see page 14).

After you've successfully gauge-swatched a substitute yarn, you'll need to figure out how much of the substitute yarn the project requires. First, find the total length of the original yarn in the pattern (multiply number of balls by yards/meters per ball). Divide this figure by the new yards/meters per ball (listed on the ball band). Round up to the next whole number. The answer is the number of balls required.

FOLLOWING CHARTS

Charts are a convenient way to follow colorwork, lace, cable and other stitch patterns at a glance. *Vogue Knitting* stitch charts utilize the universal knitting language of "symbolcraft." When knitting in the round, read charts from right to left on every round, repeating any stitch and row repeats as directed in the pattern. When knitting back and forth in rows, read charts from right to left on right side (RS) rows and from left to right on wrong side (WS) rows. Posting a self-adhesive note under your working row is an easy way to keep track of your place on a chart.

COLORWORK KNITTING

Two main types of colorwork are explored in this book.

Intarsia

Intarsia is accomplished with separate bobbins of individual colors. This method is ideal for large blocks of color or for motifs that aren't repeated close together, such as the Kid's Cotton Cap on page 84. When changing colors, always pick up the new color and wrap it around the old color to prevent holes.

Stranding

When motifs are closely placed, colorwork is accomplished by stranding along two or more colors per row, creating "floats" on the wrong side of the fabric. This technique is sometimes called Fair Isle knitting after the traditional Fair Isle patterns composed of small motifs with frequent color changes.

BLOCKING

Blocking is an all-important finishing step in the knitting process. Most hats retain their shape after pressing if the blocking stages in the instructions are followed carefully. If you plan to make several hats, invest in a head form. They can be purchased from mail order sources and are made of wood, wire or Styrofoam. If you don't have a headform an inverted bowl will make a reasonable substitute.

Wet Block Method

Place the hat on a head form and lightly dampen using a spray bottle. Allow to dry before removing.

To achieve a flat crisp edge on tams and berets, wet the knitted piece and insert a dinner plate (of appropriate size). Leave the hat to dry (with the plate in place) on a towel.

Steam Block Method

Using a head form or plate as described, steam lightly using a steam iron or steamer approximately 2"/5cm above the knitting. Do not press or it will flatten the stitches.

FINISHING TECHNIQUES

Several embellishments are used to trim the hats in this book, such as pompoms and tassels. Most hats are very simply finished at the crown by drawing a long end through the last stitches on the needles. When a hat is knit flat, an invisible back seam should be sewn from the right side.

TASSELS

Cut a piece of card board to the desired length of the tassel. Wrap yarn around the cardboard. Knot a piece of yarn tightly around one end, cut as shown, and remove the cardboard. Wrap and tie yarn around the tassel about 1"/2.5cm down from the top to secure the fringe.

YARN SYMBOLS

① Fine Weight
(29-32 stitches per 4"/10cm)
Includes baby and fingering yarns, and some of the heavier crochet cottons. The range of needle sizes is 0-4 (2-3.5mm).

② Lightweight
(25-28 stitches per 4"/10cm)
Includes sport yarn, sock yarn, UK 4-ply, and lightweight DK yarns. The range of needle sizes is 3-6 (3.25-4mm).

③ Medium Weight
(21-24 stitches per 4"/10cm)
Includes DK and worsted, the most commonly used knitting yarns. The range of needle sizes is 6-9 (4-5.5mm).

④ Medium-heavy Weight
(17-20 stitches per 4"/10cm)
Also called heavy worsted or Aran. The range of needle sizes is 8-10 (5-6mm).

⑤ Bulky Weight
(13-16 stitches per 4"/10cm)
Also called chunky. Includes heavier Icelandic yarns. The range of needle sizes is 10-11 (6-8mm).

⑥ Extra-bulky Weight
(9-12 stitches per 4"/10cm)
The heaviest yarns available. The range of needle sizes is 11 and up (8mm and up).

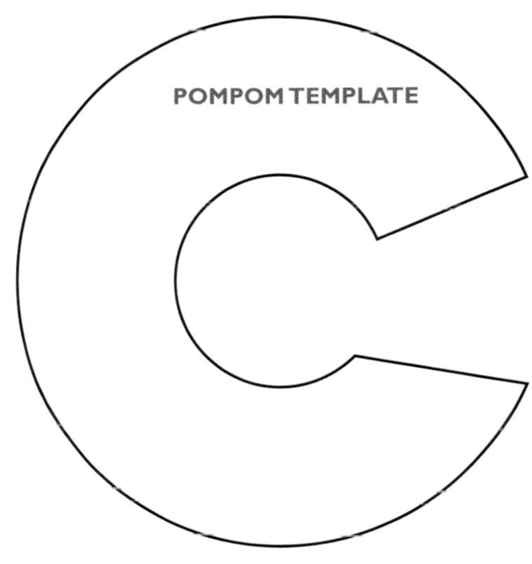

POMPOMS

1 Following the template, cut two circular pieces of cardboard.

2 Hold the two circles together and wrap the yarn tightly around the cardboard several times. Secure and carefully cut the yarn.

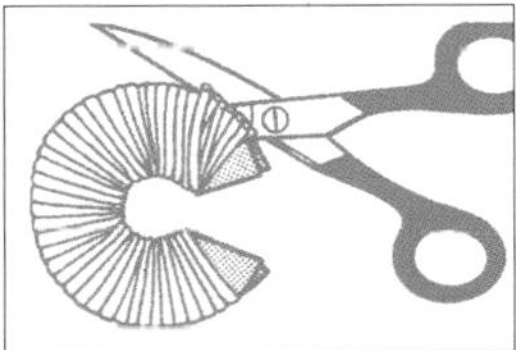

3 Tie a piece of yarn tightly between the two circles. Remove the cardboard and trim the pompom to the desired size.

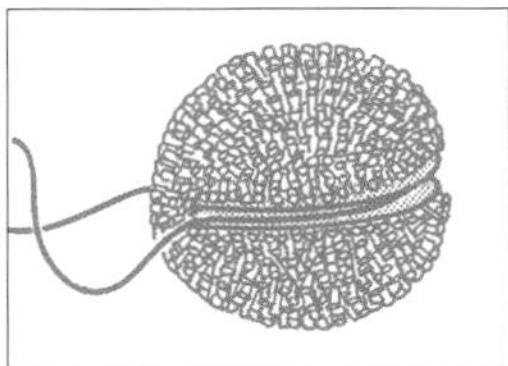

JOINING ROUNDS

CIRCULAR NEEDLES

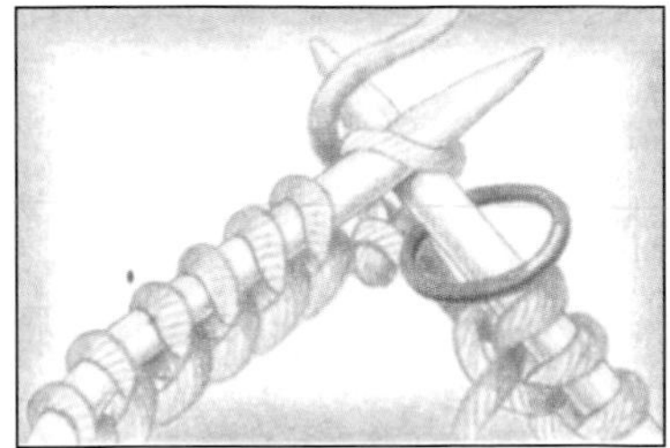

Hold the needle tip with the last cast-on stitch in your right hand and the tip with the first cast-on stitch in your left hand. Knit the first cast-on stitch, pulling the yarn tight to avoid a gap.

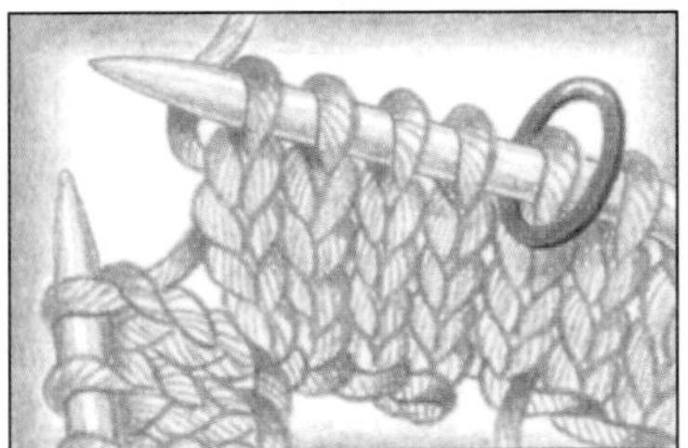

Work until you reach the marker. This completes the first round. Slip the marker to the right needle and work the next round.

TWISTED CORD

1 If you have someone to help you, insert a pencil or knitting needle through each end of the strands. If not, place one end over a doorknob and put a pencil through the other end. Turn the strands clockwise until they are tightly twisted.

2 Keeping the strands taut, fold the piece in half. Remove the pencils and allow the cords to twist onto themselves.

SHORT ROW SHAPING

"WRAP AND TURN"

1 To prevent holes in the piece and create a smooth transition, wrap a knit stitch as follows: With the yarn in back, slip the next stitch purlwise.

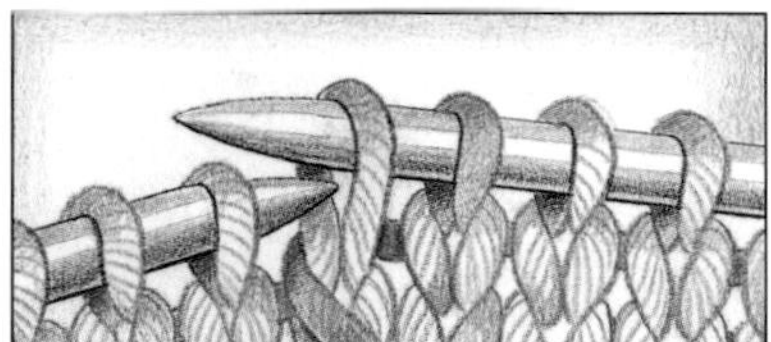

2 Move the yarn between the needle to the front of the work.

3 Slip the same stitch back to the left needle. Turn the work, bringing the yarn to the purl side between the needles. One stitch is wrapped.

4 When you have completed all the short rows, you must hide the wraps. Work to just before the wrapped stitch. Insert the right needles under the wrap and knitwise into the wrapped stitch. Knit them together.

THREE-NEEDLE BIND-OFF

1 With RS placed together, hold pieces on two parallel needles. Insert a third needle knitwise into the first stitch of each needle, and wrap the yarn around the needle as if to knit.

2 Knit these two stitches together, and slip them off the needles. *Knit the next two stitches together in the same manner.

3 Slip the first stitch on the third needle over the second stitch and off the needle. Repeat from the * in Step 2 across the row until all stitches have been bound off.

KNITTING TERMS AND ABBREVIATIONS

approx approximately

beg begin(ning)

bind off Used to finish an edge and keep stitches from unraveling. Lift the first stitch over the second, the second over the third, etc. (UK: cast off)

cast on A foundation row of stitches placed on the needle in order to begin knitting.

CC contrast color

ch chain(s)

cm centimeter(s)

cont continu(e)(ing)

dc double crochet (UK: tr-treble)

dec decrease(ing)—Reduce the stitches in a row (knit 2 together).

dpn double pointed needle(s)

foll follow(s)(ing)

g gram(s)

garter stitch Knit every row. Circular knitting: knit one round, then purl one round.

hdc half-double crochet (UK: htr-half treble)

inc increase(ing)—Add stitches in a row (knit into the front and back of a stitch).

k knit

k2tog knit 2 stitches together

lp(s) loops(s)

LH left-hand

m meter(s)

M1 make one stitch—With the needle tip, lift the strand between last stitch worked and next stitch on the left-hand needle and knit into the back of it. One stitch has been added.

MC main color

mm millimeter(s)

no stitch On some charts, "no stitch" is indicated with shaded spaces where stitches have been decreased or not yet made. In such cases, work the stitches of the chart, skipping over the "no stitch" spaces.

oz ounce(s)

p purl

p2tog purl 2 stitches together

pat pattern

pick up and knit (purl) Knit (or purl) into the loops along an edge.

pm place marker—Place or attach a loop of contrast yarn or purchased stitch marker as indicated.

rem remain(s)(ing)

rep repeat

rev St st reverse Stockinette stitch—Purl right-side rows, knit wrong-side rows. Circular knitting: purl all rounds. (UK: reverse stocking stitch)

rnd(s) round(s)

RH right-hand

RS right side(s)

sc single crochet (UK: dc - double crochet)

sk skip

SKP Slip 1, knit 1, pass slip stitch over knit 1.

sl slip—An unworked stitch made by passing a stitch from the left-hand to the right-hand needle as if to purl.

sl st slip stitch (UK: single crochet)

ssk slip, slip, knit—Slip next 2 stitches knitwise, one at a time, to right-hand needle. Insert tip of left-hand needle into fronts of these stitches from left to right. Knit them together. One stitch has been decreased.

st(s) stitch(es)

St st Stockinette stitch—Knit right-side rows, purl wrong-side rows. Circular knitting: knit all rounds. (UK: stocking stitch)

tbl through back of loop

tog together

WS wrong side(s)

w&t wrap and turn

wyif with yarn in front

wyib with yarn in back

work even Continue in pattern without increasing or decreasing. (UK: work straight)

yd yard(s)

yo yarn over—Make a new stitch by wrapping the yarn over the right-hand needle. (UK: yfwd, yon, yrn)

***** Repeat directions following * as many times as indicated.

[ ] Repeat directions inside brackets as many times as indicated.

FAIR ISLE CAP

Harvest chill chaser

For Experienced Knitters

This snug-fitting cap is knit from the top down with a spiral-increased crown and easy repetitive Fair Isle bands, giving it a distinctive style. Designed in crisp fall colors by Lynn Charlesworth.

SIZE

One size fits all. This cap is a very close-fitting style.

KNITTED MEASUREMENTS

- Head circumference 19½"/49.5cm
- Depth 7"/18cm

MATERIALS

- 1 1¾oz/50g ball (each approx 116yd/106m) of Dale of Norway *Falk* (wool ②) each in #2427 citrus (MC), #3418 orange (A), #3918 red (B), #9155 moss green (C), #5764 teal (D) and #7562 forest green (E)
- One set (4) size 6 (4mm) dpn *or size to obtain gauge*
- Size 6 (4mm) circular needle, 16"/40cm long

GAUGE

26 sts and 30 rnds to 4"/10cm over St st foll chart using size 6 (4mm) needles.
Take time to check gauge.

Note 1 When changing colors foll chart, bring new yarn from underneath working yarn to avoid holes in work. **2** Cap is knit from the top and increased down to the lower edge.

CAP

Beg at center top of cap, with one size 6 (4mm) dpn and MC, cast on 8 sts.

Rnd 1 With needle 1, k2; with needle 2, k2; with needle 3, k2, k2tog (for 3 sts on needle 3) to join rnd. Join being careful that sts are not twisted. Pm to mark beg of rnd.

Rnd 2 *Yo, k1; rep from * 6 times more—14 sts.

Rnd 3 and all odd rnds Knit.

Rnd 4 *Yo, k2; rep from * 6 times more—21 sts.

Rnd 6 *Yo, k3; rep from * 6 times more—28 sts.

Rnd 8 *Yo, k4; rep from * 6 times more—35 sts.

Rnd 10 *Yo, k5; rep from * 6 times more—42 sts.

Rnd 12 *Yo, k6; rep from * 6 times more—49 sts.

Rnd 14 *Yo, k7; rep from * 6 times more—56 sts.

Rnd 16 *Yo, k8; rep from * 6 times more—63 sts.

Rnd 18 *Yo, k9; rep from * 6 times more—70 sts.

Rnd 20 *Yo, k10; rep from * 6 times more—77 sts.

Rnd 22 *Yo, k11; rep from * 6 times more—84 sts.

Rnd 23 Knit.

Note Change to circular needle for easier working. When foll chart as described, cont to foll the inc frequency every other rnd, always making the yo in the chart background color and work the new sts into the chart pat.

Beg chart

Rnd 1 Work chart rnd 1, *yo, k12; rep from * 6 times more—91 sts.

Rnds 2, 4, 6, 8, 10 Foll chart for color pat, knit.

Rnd 3 Foll chart, *yo, k13; rep from * 6 times more—98 sts.

Rnd 5 Foll chart, *yo, k14; rep from * 6 times more—105 sts.

Rnd 7 Foll chart, *yo, k15; rep from * 6 times more—112 sts.

Rnd 9 Foll chart, *yo, k16; rep from * 6 times more—119 sts.

Rnd 11 Foll chart, *yo, k17; rep from * 6 times more—126 sts. All incs are completed.

Rnd 12 *Cont 4-st rep of chart 4 times, work last 2 sts of chart; rep from * 6 times more. Cont in this way to foll chart until row 25 of chart is completed. With MC, k1 rnd.

Band

Turn work to beg next rnd from WS of cap (that is, RS of band will be on the WS of the cap). Cont chart as established, work rnds 26-30 once. With E, purl 1 rnd (for turning ridge of band). Then foll chart, work rnds 26-30 once more. Bind off, leaving long end for sewing band in place.

FINISHING

Block cap flat. Turn up lower band to RS of cap along turning ridge. Carefully sew band in place through back lps of bound-off sts, matching st for st to cap's lower edge.

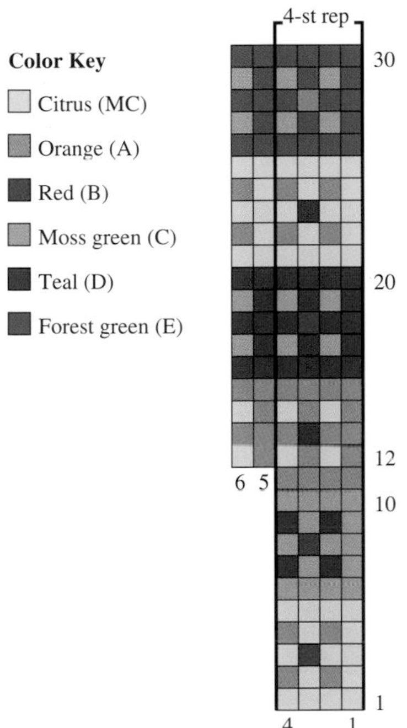
Color Key
Citrus (MC)
Orange (A)
Red (B)
Moss green (C)
Teal (D)
Forest green (E)
4-st rep
30
20
12
10
1
6 5
4 1

HERRINGBONE CLOCHE

A wayfarer's classic

For Experienced Knitters

This richly textured stitch gives a lay-flat stability to a classic cloche hat style borrowed from the flappers of the 1920's. Designed by Mari Lynn Patrick in hand-dyed yarn, which adds dimension to the stitch pattern.

SIZES

One size fits all. This cap is a standard-fitting style.

KNITTED MEASUREMENTS

- Head circumference 20"/51cm
- Depth (excluding brim) 6"/15cm

MATERIALS

- 2 1¾oz/50g hanks (each approx 114yd/m) of Koigu Wool Designs *Kersti Merino* (wool ③) in #1230 dk green
- One pair size 6 (4mm) needles *or size to obtain gauge*
- One pair size 7 (4.5mm) needles for casting on only
- Size 6 (4mm) circular needle 20"/50cm long
- 1 yd/1m of leather cord

GAUGE

30 sts and 26 rows to 4"/10cm over herringbone pat st using size 6 (4mm) needles.

Take time to check gauge.

HERRINGBONE PATTERN STITCH

(over an odd number of sts)

Row 1 (WS) *P2tog and leave sts on LH needle, purl first st again, drop both sts tog from LH needle; rep from *, end p1.

Row 2 (RS) *Sl 1 wyib, k1, with LH needle raise up sl st slightly, pull RH needle through raised st like a psso but do not drop raised st from LH needle, k into back lp of raised st and drop from needle; rep from *, end k1.

Rep rows 1 and 2 for herringbone pat st.

HAT

Side Crown Section

(make 2)

With size 7 (4.5mm) needles, cast on 55 sts. Change to size 6 (4mm) needles and work in herringbone pat st for 4 rows.

****Dec row 1 (WS)** P2tog (for dec 1 st); rep from * of row 1 of pat, end p1.

Dec row 2 (RS), k2tog (for dec 1 st); rep from * of row 2 to last 2 sts, k2tog (for dec 1 st).

Dec row 3 (WS) Rep from * of row 1 to last 2 sts, p2tog (for dec 1 st)—4 sts dec'd for 51 sts. Work even for 1 row **. Rep between **'s 3 times more—39 sts.

+**Dec row 4 (WS)** [P2tog] twice; rep from * of row 1 to end.

Dec row 5 (RS) [K2tog] twice; rep from * of row 2 to end +.

Rep between +'s 5 times more—15 sts.

Dec row 6 [P2tog] twice, rep from * of row 1 to last 5 sts, [p2tog] twice, p1.

Dec row 7 [K2tog] twice, rep from * of row 2 to last 5 sts, [k2tog] twice, k1.

Next row [P2tog] 3 times, p1.

Next row SK2P, k1, turn. Bind off 1 st and fasten off.

Center Crown Section

(make 1)

With size 7 (4.5mm) needles, cast on 59 sts. Change to size 6 (4mm) needles and work in herringbone pat st for 4 rows. Then cont as for side crown section, beg at ** and working up to Dec row 4—43 sts. Rep between +'s a total of 5 times—23 sts.

Then rep dec rows 6 and 7 twice—7 sts.

Next row (WS) [P2tog] 3 times, p1.

Next row SK2P, k1, turn. Bind off 1 st and fasten off.

Sew the 2 side crown sections to center crown section leaving back seam open.

BRIM

With RS facing and size 6 (4mm) circular needle, pick up and k 175 sts evenly around lower edge of joined crown pieces.

Row 1 (WS) Work row 1 of herringbone pat st.

Row 2 (RS) Work 10 sts, yo, work 34 sts, yo, [work 44 sts, yo] twice, work 34 sts, yo, work 9 sts.

Row 3 (WS) Work row 1 of pat st, working a p2tog into yo of previous row plus the next st, then pick up 1 st in row below and lift to LH needle to make next p2tog—185 sts. The 5 yo's of previous row will become 10 extra sts or 2 sts will be added for each yo in this way.

Row 4 Work 6 sts, yo, work 44 sts, yo, work 38 sts, yo, work 46 sts, yo, work 44 sts, yo, work 7 sts.

Row 5 Rep row 3—195 sts. Cont to inc in this way, adding 5 yo's every RS row (not directly over yo's of previous inc row) and a total of 10 sts every WS row 8 times more, AT SAME TIME, shape back brim with short rows beg on row 8 as foll:

Short row 8 Working 5 spaced yo's as before, work to last 7 sts, w&t.

Short row 9 Working 10 incs as before, work to last 7 sts, w&t.

Short row 10 Working 5 spaced yo's work to last 13 sts, w&t.

Short row 11 Working 10 incs as before,

work to last 13 sts, w&t.

Short row 12 Working 5 spaced yo's, work to last 19 sts, w&t.

Short row 13 Working 10 incs as before, work to last 19 sts, w&t.

Short row 14 Working 5 spaced yo's, work to last 25 sts, w&t.

Short row 15 Working 10 incs as before, work to last 25 sts, w&t.

Row 16 Working 5 spaced yo's, work across all sts to end, working into wrapped sts to close up holes.

Row 17 Working 10 incs as before, work all sts to end, working into wrapped sts to close up holes.

Next row (RS) Bind off sts as foll: *p1, p2tog; bind off 1 st; rep from * across.

FINISHING

Block brim flat very carefully. Do not block rest of hat. Sew back brim seam. Draw leather cord through hat at brim pick-up line.

WAVY CABLED CAP

Hot tamale!

For Experienced Knitters

Dimensional wavy cables are worked against a background of seed stitch for contrasting texture. The cables cleverly diminish along the crown to end in a small top knot; twisted cord tassels are attached to the patterned earflaps.

SIZES

One size fits all. This cap is a loose-fitting style.

KNITTED MEASUREMENTS

- Head circumference 21"/53cm
- Depth (excluding earflaps) 8"/20.5cm

MATERIALS

- 2 1¾oz/50g balls (each approx 131yd/120m) of K1C2, LLC *Crème Brulée* (wool ③) in #359 red
- One pair each sizes 3 and 5 (3.25 and 3.74mm) needles *or size to obtain gauge*
- Cable needle (cn)

GAUGE

28 sts and 30 rows to 4"/10cm over chart pat using size 5 (3.74mm) needles.
Take time to check gauge.

STITCH GLOSSARY

4-ST RPC
(This cable st is not used in chart pats)Sl next st to cn and hold to *back*, k3, p1 from cn.

5-ST RPC Sl next 2 sts to cn and hold to *back*, k3, p2 from cn.

5-ST LPC Sl next 3 sts to cn and hold to *front*, p2, k3 from cn.

6-ST LC Sl next 3 sts to cn and hold to *front*, k3, k3 from cn.

6-ST RC Sl next 3 sts to cn and hold to *back*, k3, k3 from cn.

CAP

First earflap

With size 5 (3.75mm) needles, cast on 15 sts. Beg foll earflap chart as foll:

Row 1 (RS) Inc 1 st in first st, p1; 5-st LPC, [k1, p1] 3 times, inc 1 st in next st, k1 17 sts.

Row 2 Inc 1 st in first st, [p1, k1] 4 times, p3, k3, inc 1 st in next st, k1—19 sts.

Row 3 Inc 1 st in first st, p5, k3, [k1, p1] 3 times, k2, inc 1 st in next st, k1—21 sts.

Row 4 P4, [k1, p1] 4 times, p2, k6, p1.

Row 5 Inc 1 st in first st, p6, k4, [p1, k1] 3 times, k2, inc 1 st in next st, k1—23 sts.

Row 6 P5, [k1, p1] 4 times, p2, k6, p2.

Row 7 Inc 1 st in first st, k1, p4, 5-st RPC, [k1, p1] 3 times, k4, inc 1 st in next st, k1—25 sts.

Row 8 P6, [k1, p1] 5 times, p2, k4, p3.

Row 9 Inc 1 st in first st, k2, p2, 5-ST RPC, [k1, p1] 3 times, k1, 5-ST RPC, k1, inc 1 st in next st, k1—27 sts.

Row 10 K1, p3, k2, p3, [k1, p1] 5 times, p2, k2, p3, k1.

Row 11 Inc 1 st in first st, k3, 5-ST RPC, [k1, p1] 3 times, k1, 5-ST RPC, p2, k2, inc 1 st in next st, p1—29 sts.

Row 12 P1, k1, p3, k4, p3, [k1, p1] 5 times, p5, k1, p1.

Row 13 Inc 1 st in first st, k1, 6-ST RC,

[k1, p1] 3 times, k1, 5-st RPC, p4, k3, inc 1 st in next st, k1—31 sts.

Cont to foll earflap chart in this way on 31 sts through row 32. Cut yarn. Leave these sts on a holder.

Second Earflap

Work as for first earflap. Do not cut yarn.

Next row (RS) At beg of row cast on 11 sts, then [p1, k1] 3 times, 5-ST RPC, * k6, p2, 5-ST RPC, [k1, p1] 3 times, k1, 5-ST RPC, k6 *, turn. Cast on 69 sts, then working across the 31 sts of first earflap from holder, rep between *'s, turn. Cast on 10 sts—152 sts.

Beg panel pat

Foundation row (WS) K1, working from left to right, work row 24 of panel pat chart, working 25-st rep a total of 6 times, k1. Beg and end with k1, work rows 1-24 of panel pat as established until piece measures approx 6"/15cm from beg of cap above earflaps, ending with row 20 of panel pat chart.

Shape top

Note Cont to work a k1 selvage st at each end of row (not included in the instructions below) and work as foll:

Row 1 (RS) [K1, p3tog, k1, p1, k1, 6-ST LC, k3, p4, 5-ST RPC] 6 times.

Row 2 [P1, k1, p3, k4, p9, (k1, p1) twice, k1] 6 times.

Row 3 [P3tog, 5-ST RPC, k6, p2, 5-st RPC, k1, p1] 6 times—128 sts.

Row 4 *[P1, k1] twice, p3, k2, p6, k2, p3, k1; rep from * 5 times more.

Row 5 Work 4-ST RPC, *p2, k6, 5-ST RPC, p3tog, 5-ST RPC; rep from * to last 17 sts, p2, k6, 5-ST RPC, p3tog, p1—116 sts.

Row 6 [P1, k1] twice, *p9, k4, p3, k3; rep from * to last 15 sts, p9, k3, p3.

Row 7 K3, p3tog, *k3, 6-ST RC, p3, k3, p1, p3tog; rep from * to last 13 sts, k3, 6-ST RC, p3tog, p1—102 sts.

Row 8 K2, *p9, k2, p3, k3; rep from * to last 13 sts, p9, k1, p3.

Row 9 K3, p1, *k9, p3tog, k3, p2; rep from * to last 11 sts, k9, p2tog—91 sts.

Row 10 K1, *p9, k2, p3, k1; rep from * to last 13 sts, end p9, k1, p3.

Row 11 K3, k2tog, k8, *p1, 5-ST LPC, k9; rep from * to last st, p1—90 sts.

Row 12 K1, *p12, k3; rep from * to last 12 sts, p12.

Row 13 *[Sl next 3 sts to cn and hold to back, k3, then k2tog, k1 from cn] twice, p3; rep from *, end p1—78 sts.

Row 14 K1, *p10, k3; rep from * to last 10 sts, p10.

Row 15 *K10, p3tog; rep from * to last 11 sts, k10, p1—68 sts.

Row 16 *K1, p10; rep from * to end.

Row 17 *K10, p1; rep from * to end.

Row 18 Rep row 16.

Row 19 *[Sl next 3 sts to cn and hold to *back*, k2, k3tog from cn] twice, p1; rep from * to end—44 sts.

Row 20 *K1, p6; rep from * to end.

Row 21 *K2tog, k2, SKP, p1; rep from * to end—32 sts.

Row 22 *K1, p4; rep from * to end.

Row 23 *K3tog tbl, SKP; rep from * to end—14 sts. Beg with a purl row, work 7 rows in St st. Cut yarn leaving a long end for sewing seam, and draw through rem 14 sts, draw up tightly and secure.

FINISHING

Block flat to measurements.

Lower Edging

With smaller needles and RS facing, pick up and k sts around lower edge as foll: 9 sts along left back edge, 23 sts along one side of earflap, 15 sts along cast-on edge of earflap, 23 sts along other side of earflap, 60 sts along front cast-on edge, 23 sts along side of earflap, 15 sts along cast-on edge of earflap, 23 sts along other side of earflap, 9 sts along right back edge—200 sts. K2 rows. Bind off knitwise.

Twisted Cord

(make 2)

Cut 6 strands of yarn, 23"/59cm long. Make a twisted cord and attach to each earflap. Sew back seam.

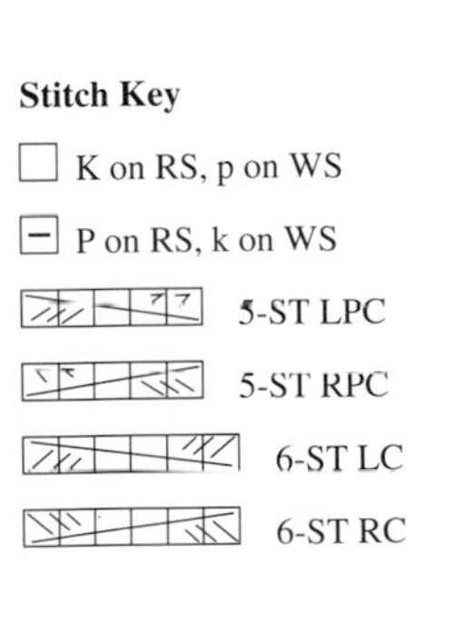

PANEL PATTERN CHART

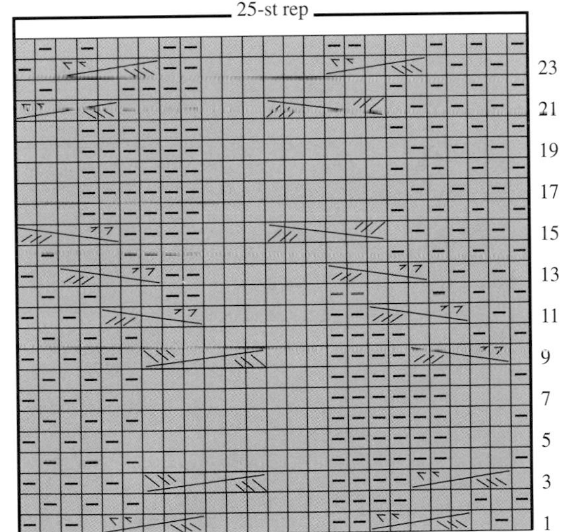

EARFLAP CHART

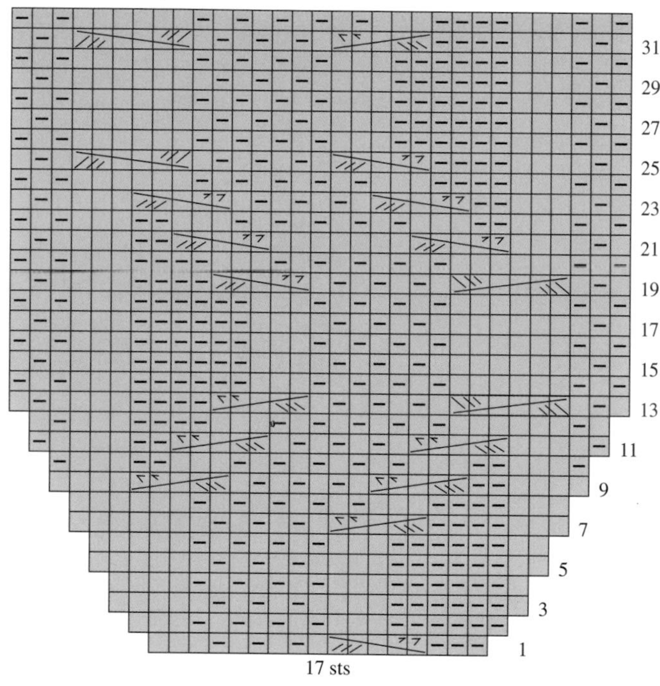

Stitch Key

- K on RS, p on WS
- P on RS, k on WS
- 5-ST LPC
- 5-ST RPC
- 6-ST LC
- 6-ST RC

SCOTTIE HAT

A girl's best friend

For Intermediate Knitters

Fun, furry Scottie dogs with ribbon ties march around this hat. Designed by Maggie Branch in sizes for little girls and their grown-up friends it features a double rolled brim to complete the look.

SIZES

Instructions are written for Child's size 4-6 (18"/45.5cm). Changes for Woman's size Small/Medium (21-22"/53-56cm) are in parentheses. Shown in Woman's size Small/Medium (21-22"/53-56cm). This hat is a close-fitting style.

KNITTED MEASUREMENTS

- Head circumference 17 (19)"/43 (48)cm
- Depth (with lower edge rolled) 7¼ (8½)"/18.5 (21.5)cm

MATERIALS

- 2 1¾oz/50g balls (each approx 82yd/75m) of Garnstudio/Aurora Yarns *Alaska* (wool ④) in #03 grey (MC)
- 1 1¾oz/50g ball (each approx 132yd/120m) of Garnstudio/Aurora Yarns *Pelliza* (wool/acrylic/polyamide ③) in #10 black (A)
- One set (5) size 7 (4.5mm) dpn *or size to obtain gauge*
- 1 yd/1m .5mm wide red ribbon

GAUGE

19 sts and 26 rows to 4"/10cm over St st using MC and size 7 (4.5mm) dpn.
Take time to check gauge.

Notes 1 Use double strand A when working chart. **2** When changing colors foll chart, twist new yarn around working yarn to avoid holes in work.

HAT

Beg at lower edge with MC, cast on 81 (90) sts. Divide sts on 4 needles with 20 sts on first 3 needles and 21 sts on needle 4 for Child's size; 22 sts on needles 1 and 3 and 23 sts on needles 2 and 4 for Woman's size. Join, being careful not to twist sts and pm to mark beg of rnd. K10 rnds, p4 rnds for double rolled edge. Then cont in St st, k5 rnds.

Beg chart pat

Rnd 1 (RS) *With MC, k5 (3), work 15 sts (with double strand A) of chart pat; rep from * 3 (4) times more, end k1 (0) MC. Cont to foll chart in this way through rnd 15. Then cont in St st with MC only for 1¾ (3)"/4.5 (7.5)cm.

Shape crown

Rnd 1 *K7 (8), k2tog; rep from * 8 times more—72 (81) sts.

Rnd 2 Knit.

Rnd 3 *K6 (7), k2tog; rep from * 8 times more—63 (72) sts.

Rnd 4 Knit.

Rnd 5 *K5 (6), k2tog; rep from * 8 times more—54 (63) sts.

Rnd 6 Knit.

Rnd 7 *K4 (5), k2tog; rep from * 8 times more—45 (54) sts.

Rnd 8 Knit.

Rnd 9 *K3 (4), k2tog; rep from * 8 times more—36 (45) sts.

Rnd 10 Knit.

For Child's size only

Rnd 11 [K2tog] 18 times—18 sts.

Rnd 12 [K3tog] 6 times—6 sts.

For Woman's size only

Rnd 11 *K3, k2tog; rep from * 8 times more—36 sts.

Rnd 12 Knit.

Rnd 13 [K2tog] 18 times—18 sts.

Rnd 14 [K3tog] 6 times—6 sts.

Both sizes

Change to double strand A and work rem 6 sts even for 1"/2.5cm.

Next rnd [K2tog] 3 times. K3tog and fasten off.

FINISHING

Block lightly being sure to keep lower edge rolled.

Cut 4 (5) 7"/18cm lengths of ribbon and tie around the neck of each Scottie dog around. Tie ribbon in bows as shown.

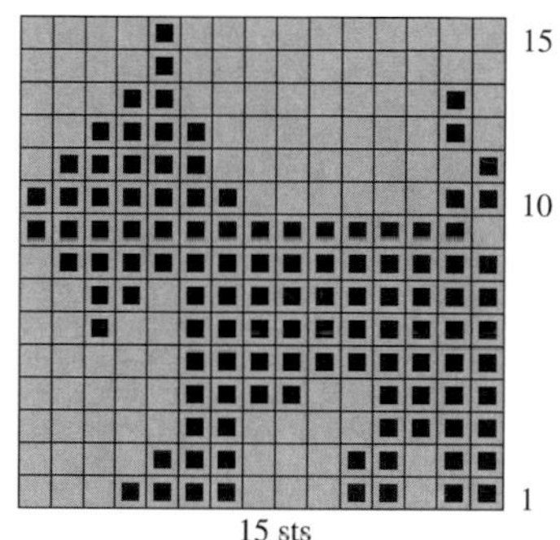

Color Key

Grey (MC)

Black (A), double strand

RIBBED CAP

Artist's palette

One ball of hand-dyed yarn plays out beautifully in a symphony of stripes in this uniquely colored wool yarn. Designed by Carla Scott, this cap can be knit straight and seamed, or knit in the round on double-pointed needles.

SIZE

One size fits all. This cap is a standard-fitting style.

KNITTED MEASUREMENTS

- Head circumference (slightly stretched) 21"/53cm
- Depth 7"/18cm

MATERIALS

- 1 1¾oz/50g ball (each approx 108yd/100m) of Noro/KFI *Kureyon* (wool ④) in #80 turquoise or #51 charcoal or #55 brown or #102 pink
- One pair size 8 (5mm) straight needles *or size to obtain gauge*
- 1 set (4) size 8 (5mm) dpn *or size to obtain gauge*

GAUGE

20 sts and 28 rows/rnds to 4"/10cm over k4, p4 rib using size 8 (5mm) straight needles OR dpn.

Take time to check gauge.

STRAIGHT NEEDLES

K4, P4 RIB PATTERN

Row 1 (RS) K2, *p4, k4; rep from *, end last rep k2 instead of k4.

Row 2 K the knit and p the purl sts.

Rep row 2 for k4, p4 rib pat.

DOUBLE POINTED NEEDLES

K4, P4 RIB PATTERN

Rnd 1 *K4, p4; rep from * around.

Rep rnd 1 for k4, p4 rib pat.

CAP

Straight Knitting

With straight needles, cast on 106 sts.

Row 1 (RS) K1 (selvage st), work in k4, p4 rib pat to last st, k1 (selvage st). Work in k4, p4 rib pat as established (with k1 selvage st each side of row) until piece measures 6"/15cm from beg, end with a WS row.

Shape top

Row 1 (RS) K3, *p1, p2tog, p1, k1, k2tog, k1; rep from * to last 3 sts, end k3—81 sts.

Row 2 K the knit and p the purl sts.

Row 3 K3, *p2tog, p1, k2tog, k1; rep from * to last 3 sts, k3—56 sts.

Row 4 K the knit and p the purl sts.

Row 5 K3, *p2tog, k2; rep from * to last 3 sts, k3—43 sts.

Row 6 K the knit and p the purl sts.

Row 7 K1, *k2tog, p1; rep from * to last 3 sts, k2tog, k1—29 sts.

Row 8 K1, *p1, p2tog; rep from *, end k1—20 sts.

Row 9 [K2tog] 10 times—10 sts*. Cut yarn leaving a long end for sewing back seam. Pull through rem 10 sts and draw up tightly to secure. Sew back seam.

FINISHING

Do not block or flatten rib.

I-cord style

To make I-cord style shown, work to end of row 9*.

Next row P3tog, [p2tog] twice, p3tog—4 sts. Using 2 dpn, work I-cord as foll: *k3, slide sts to beg of needle to work sts from same position. Bring yarn around from back and rep from * until I-cord measures 6"/15cm. Bind off. Knot as shown. Sew back seam.

CIRCULAR KNITTING

With dpn, cast on 104 sts and divide sts on 3 needles with 34 sts on needle 1, 36 sts on needle 2 and 34 sts on needle 3. Join, being careful not to twist sts and pm to mark beg of rnd. Work in k4, p4 rib pat in rnds for 6"/15cm.

Shape top

Rnd 1 *K1, k2tog, k1, p1, p2tog, p1; rep from * around—78 sts.

Rnd 2 K the knit sts and p the purl sts.

Rnd 3 *K2tog, k1, p2tog, p1; rep from * around—52 sts.

Rnd 4 K the knit and p the purl sts.

Rnd 5 *K2, p2tog; rep from * around—39 sts.

Rnd 6 K the knit and p the purl sts.

Rnd 7 *K2tog, p1, rep from * around—26 sts.

Rnd 8 K2, *k2tog, k1; rep from * around—18 sts.

Rnd 9 [K2tog] 9 times—9 sts. Cut yarn leaving an end for sewing top. Pull through rem 9 sts and draw up tightly to secure. Fasten off.

FINISHING

Do not block or flatten rib.

FLOWER TOPPED STRIPED CAP

Making waves

For Intermediate Knitters

This wonderfully patterned cap is knit in muted tweed yarns in varying pointelle point, ridge and ripple patterns to give a unique edge. Designed by Fiona Ellis.

SIZES

Instructions are written for size Medium (22"/56cm). Changes for size Large/X-Large (23-24"/58.5-61cm) are in parentheses. Shown in size Large/X-Large. This cap is a very loose-fitting style.

KNITTED MEASUREMENTS

- Head circumference 20 (22½)"/51 (57)cm
- Depth 8½"/21.5cm

MATERIALS

- 1 1¾oz/50g ball (each approx 76yd/70m) of Bergère de France/Skacel Collection *Irland* (wool/acrylic/rayon ④) each in #092 lt blue (A), #133 dk blue (B) and #379 green (C).
- 1 set (4) size 7 (4.5mm) dpn *or size to obtain gauge*
- Size 7 (4.5mm) circular needle, 16"/40cm long
- Size G/6 (4.5mm) crochet hook

GAUGE

19 sts and 25 rows/rnds to 4"/10cm over St st using size 7 (4.5mm) needles.

Take time to check gauge.

CAP

With circular needle and A, cast on 96 (108) sts. Join and working in rnds, k1 rnd, p1 rnd. Change to B.

Beg wave pat

Rnd 1 *K1, yo, k4, SK2P, k4, yo; rep from * 7 (8) times more.

Rnd 2 and all even rnds Purl.

Note Be sure to p the final yo from rnd 1 or the st count will not remain the same.

Rnd 3 K2, *yo, k3, SK2P, k3, yo, k3; rep from *, ending last rep k1 instead of k3.

Rnd 5 K3, *yo, k2, SK2P, k2, yo, k5; rep from * ending last rep k2 instead of k5.

Rnd 7 K4, *yo, k1, SK2P, k1, yo, k7; rep from * ending last rep k3 instead of k7.

Rnd 9 K5, *yo, SK2P, yo, k9; rep from * ending last rep k4 instead of k9.

Rnd 10 Purl.

**Change to A and k1 rnd, p1 rnd (for garter ridge). Change to C.

Beg wave pat

Rnd 1 Knit.

Rnd 2 P3, [k7, p5] 7 (8) times, k7, p2.

Rnd 3 K2, *p2, k5, p2, k3; rep from * ending last rep k1, instead of k3.

Rnd 4 K3, *p2, k3, p2, k5; rep from * ending last rep k2 instead of k5.

Rnd 5 K4, [p5, k7] 7 (8) times, p5, k3. Change to A and k1 rnd, p1 rnd. Change to B and work rnds 1-5 of wave pat once, rnds 2-5 once. Rep from ** once more. Change to A and k1 rnd, p1 rnd.

Shape crown

Change to C.

Rnd 1 and all odd rnds Knit.

Rnd 2 *K1, k2tog, k11 (13), k2tog tbl; rep from * around—84 (96) sts.

Rnd 4 *K1, k2tog, k9 (11), k2tog tbl; rep form * around—72 (84) sts.

Rnd 6 *K1, k2tog, k7 (9), k2tog tbl; rep from * around—60 (72) sts.

Rnd 8 *K1, k2tog, k5 (7) k2tog tbl; rep from * around—48 (60) sts. Change to dpn to accommodate the fewer sts.

Rnd 10 *K1, k2tog, k 3 (5), k2tog tbl; rep from * around—36 (48) sts.

Rnd 12 *K1, k2tog, k1 (3), k2tog tbl; rep from * around—24 (36) sts.

Size medium only

Rnd 14 K2tog, pass last st from previous rnd over this st, k1, *SK2P, k1; rep from *, omitting the k1 on last rep—12 sts.

Rnd 16 [K3tog] 4 times—4 sts rem.

Size large/X-large only

Rnd 14 *K1, k2tog, k1, k2tog tbl; rep from * around—24 sts.

Rnd 16 K2tog, pass last st from previous rnd over this st, k1, *SK2P, k1; rep from *, omitting the k1 on last rep —12 sts.

Rnd 17 [K3tog] 4 times—4 sts rem.

Both sizes

Cut yarn and pull through rem 4 sts and draw up tightly to secure top.

FINISHING

Block lightly, pinning lower edge to form points.

FLOWER

With crochet hook and A, ch 50.

Rnd 1 Sc in 2nd ch for hook and in each ch to end. Fasten off. With B, work another ch in same way. Fold A ch into 3 lps and fasten to top of cap. Fold B ch into 3 lps and fasten in an alternating flower style on top of A lps.

SNOWFLAKE BERET

Tasseled "Tam o' shanter"

For Experienced Knitters

Six wedge-shaped stitch repeats form the foundation of this snowflake pattern beret designed by Donna Druchunas. Embroidery, twisted cord ribbing at the edge and a braided and corded tassel make up this unique design.

SIZE

One size fits all. This beret is a loose-fitting style.

KNITTED MEASUREMENTS

- Head circumference 19"/48cm
- Diameter 10"/25.5cm

MATERIALS

- 2 1¾oz/50g balls (each approx 98yd/90m) of Karabella Yarns *Aurora 8* (wool ③) in #1364 camel
- One each sizes 4 and 7 (3.5 and 4.5mm) circular needle, 20"/50cm long *or size to obtain gauge*
- One set (4) size 7 (4.5mm) dpn
- Cable needle (cn)
- Stitch markers

GAUGE

18 sts and 28 rows/rnds to 4"/10cm over St st using larger circular needles.
Take time to check gauge.

BERET

With smaller circular needle, cast on 96 sts loosely. Join being careful not to twist sts on needle and pm to mark beg of rnd.

Rnd 1 *K1 tbl, p1; rep from * around.

Rep rnd 1 for twisted k1, p1 rib for 4 rnds more.

Next (inc) rnd Cont in twisted rib as established, work as foll: *rib 2 sts, M1 purlwise, [rib 3 sts, M1 purlwise] twice, rib 2 sts, M1 purlwise, rib 3 sts, M1 purlwise, rib 3 sts; rep from * 5 times more—126 sts. Change to larger circular needle.

Beg chart pat

Set-up rnd Remove marker, *k4, (replace marker for new beg of rnd), p6, k1 tbl, p6, k4; rep from * (without markers) 5 times more. Then working 21-st rep 6 times, work rnds 1-9 of chart 3 times.

Shape crown

Changing to dpn when there are too few sts to fit on circular needle, work rnds 1-29 of chart—6 sts rem. Pull yarn through rem 6 sts and draw up tightly and secure.

FINISHING

Wash finished beret in lukewarm water and mild soap. Wring out water gently. Insert a 10"/25.5cm plate into beret and allow to dry.

Embroidery

Working into 3 alternating 8-st St st segments, embroider 2 flowers in each of these segments in lazy daisy st foll embroidery chart.

Tassel

Wind yarn 25 times around a 4"/10cm piece of cardboard. Set aside for tassel.

BRAID

Cut 6 strands of yarn 15"/38cm long. Using tapestry needle, draw these strands through wrapped yarn at top of cardboard. Using 2 strands of yarn for each section, braid yarn tightly. Cut a 10"/26cm piece of yarn and wrap tightly around tassel strands at approx 1"/2.5cm from top end of tassel. Cut other cord to form tassel. Trim tassel and fasten with braid to top of beret.

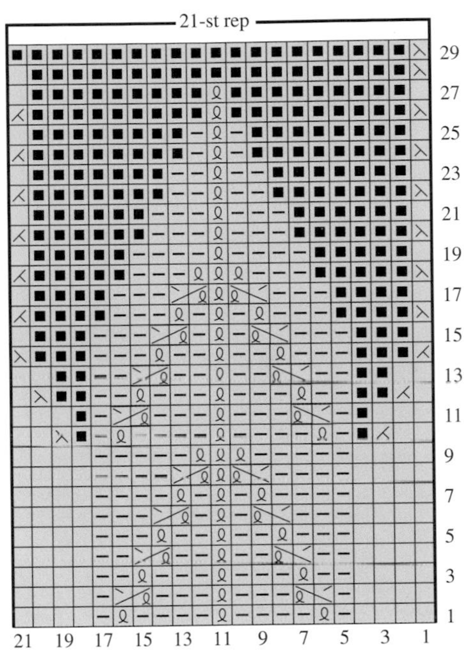

embroidery chart

Stitch Key

- K on RS, p on WS
- P on RS, k on WS
- K1tbl
- Ssk
- K2tog
- Slip one st to cn and hold to *back*, k1tbl, p1 from cn
- Slip one st to cn and hold to *front*, p1, k1tbl, k1 from cn
- No stitch

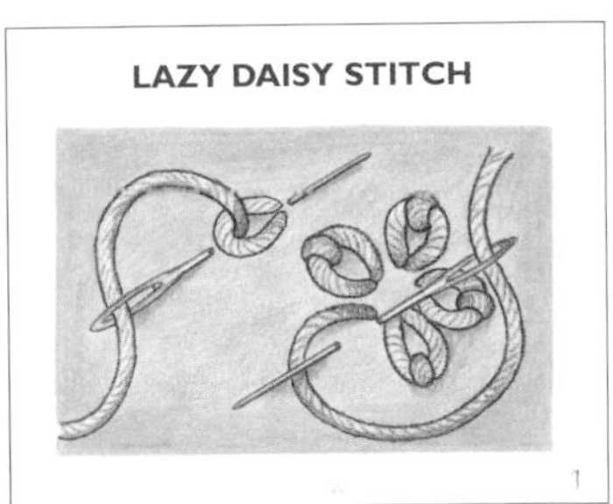

BIRDSEYE ROLLED CAP

Winter warm-up

For Intermediate Knitters

Neon bright colors are worked with black in a one-by-one birdseye stitch that gives thermal depth to this simple kid's cap style. Designed by Jil Eaton.

SIZES

Instructions are written for Infant's size 12 months. Changes for size Toddler 2-4 and Child's size 6 are in parentheses. This cap is a standard-fitting style.

KNITTED MEASUREMENTS

- Head circumference 17 (18, 19)"/43 (45.5, 48)cm
- Depth (with edge rolled) 6 (6, 7¼)"/15 (15, 18.5)cm

MATERIALS

- 1 1¾oz/50g skein (each approx 48yd/44m) of Brown Sheep Yarn Co. *Lamb's Pride Worsted* (wool/nylon ④) in #M05 black (MC), #M120 lime (A), #M78 turquoise (B) and #M81 red (C)
- 1 set (5) size 8 (5mm) dpn *or size to obtain gauge*
- Size 8 (5mm) circular needle, 16"/40cm long

GAUGE

22 sts and 20 rnds to 4"/10cm over birdseye pat st using 2 colors and size 8 (5mm) needles. *Take time to check gauge.*

BIRDSEYE PATTERN STITCH

(even number of sts)

Rnds 1 and 3 *K1 with MC, k1 with A; rep from * around.

Rnds 2 and 4 *K1 with A, k1 with MC; rep from * around

Rnds 5 and 7 *K1 with MC, k1 with B; rep from * around

Rnds 6 and 8 *K1 with B, k1 with MC; rep from * around

Rnds 9 and 11 *K1 with MC, k1 with C; rep from * around

Rnds 10 and 12 *K1 with C, k1 with MC; rep from * around.

Rep these 12 rnds for birdseye pat st.

CAP

Beg at lower edge with circular needle and A, cast on 84 (90, 96) sts. Join to work in rnds. Pm to mark beg of rnd. Work in St st (k every rnd) for 9 rnds, inc 8 sts evenly across last rnd—92 (98, 104) sts. P next rnd. Beg with rnd 1, work in birdseye pat st for a total of 24 (24, 28) rnds and a total of 6 (6, 7) stripes.

Shape top

Note Cont to work birdseye pat st and stripe pat in next consecutive color.

Rnd 1 *Work 8 sts, [k2tog] twice; rep from * 6 (7, 7) times more, work 8 (2, 8) sts—78 (82, 88) sts.

Rnd 2 Work even in pat.

Rnd 3 *Work 6 sts, [k2tog] twice; rep from * 6 (7, 7) times more, work 8 (2, 8) sts—64 (66, 72) sts.

Rnd 4 Work even in pat.

Rnd 5 *Work 4 sts, [k2tog] twice; rep from * 6 (7, 7) times more, work 8 (2, 8) sts—50 (50, 56) sts.

Rnd 6 [K2tog] 25 (25, 28) times—25 (25, 28) sts.

Rnd 7 [K2tog] 12 (12, 14) times, k1 (1, 0)—13 (13, 14) sts. Cut yarn and pull through rem sts and draw up tightly to secure. Fasten off.

FINISHING

Block lightly, allowing lower edge to roll up without pressing

TASSELED CAP

It's hip to be square

Four easy panels are worked in different directions to give this simple cap its distinctive style. A ribbed band and tassels at the corners finish off this unisex design by Norah Gaughan.

SIZES

Instructions are written for Unisex size X-Small/Small (20"-21"/51-53cm). Changes for sizes Medium (22"/56cm) and Large/X-Large (23-24"/58.5-61cm) are in parentheses. Shown in size X-Small/Small. This cap is a close-fitting style.

KNITTED MEASUREMENTS

- Head circumference 19 (20, 21)"/48 (51, 53)cm
- Depth 7¼"/18.5cm

MATERIALS

- 1 5.25oz/150g hanks (each approx 246yd/227m) of JCA/Artful Yarns *Jazz* in #55 (wool/alpaca ④)
- One pair size 8 (5mm) needles or size to obtain gauge
- Sizes 6 and 8 (4 and 5mm) circular needle, 16"/40cm long

GAUGE

17 sts and 24 rows to 4"/10cm over St st using larger needles.
Take time to check gauge.

Note Pick-up sts on the WS as indicated to form the decorative ridges shown in this cap.

SIDE PANEL

(make 2)
With larger straight needles, cast on 18 sts. Work even for 16 rows or 2¾"/7cm.
Dec row (RS) K1, k2tog, k to last 3 sts, ssk, k1. Rep dec row every 6th row once, every 4th row once, every 2nd row 4 times—4 sts. P1 row then bind off.

CENTER BAND

(2 pieces)
Working from WS (for ridge) along side edges of one side panel (the beg and the end of rows) with larger circular needle, pick up and k 54 sts evenly around entire shaped side panel. (That is, pick up and k 25 sts along one side edge, 4 sts in bound-off sts at top and 25 sts along other side edge). Working back and forth in rows, work in St st for 3 (3½, 4)"/7.5 (9, 10)cm. Leave sts on hold. Work other center band with second side panel in same way.

FINISHING

With two pieces tog so that WS is facing and using a 3rd needle, work 3-needle bind-off with decorative seam on outside.

Lower band

With smaller circular needle working from WS, pick up and k 92 (96, 104) sts evenly along lower edge. Join and work in k2, p2 rib for 1¼"/3cm. Bind off in rib.

Tassels

(make 2)

Wind yarn 50 times around a 3"/7.5cm cardboard. Tie tassel at ½"/1.5cm from one end and cut other end.

MULTICOLOR EARFLAP CAP

Mountain top mosaic

For Experienced Knitters

Repetitive cross motifs in multiple bright colors against black with a four-part angular crown make this earflap cap especially fun to knit. Based on caps in the tradition of Peruvian textiles worn in the Andes, this cap is designed by Deborah Newton.

SIZE

One size fits all. This cap is a loose-fitting style.

FINISHED MEASUREMENTS

- Head circumference 20"/51cm
- Depth (excluding earflap) 10"/25.5cm

MATERIALS

- 1 1¾oz/50g skein (each approx 138yd/123m) of Classic Elite Yarns *Waterspun* (wool ④) each in #5013 black (MC), #5051 gold (A), #5057 periwinkle blue (B), #5019 hot pink (C), #5031 turquoise (D), #5085 orange (E) and #5074 leaf green (F)
- One set (5) size 7 (4.5mm) dpn *or size to obtain gauge*
- One pair size 7 (4.5mm) straight needles

GAUGE

21 sts and 24 rows/rnds to 4"/10cm over St st using size 7 (4.5mm) needles.
Take time to check gauge.

Note When changing colors foll chart, bring new yarn from underneath working yarn to avoid holes in work.

CAP

Beg at lower edge with dpn and MC, cast on 100 sts. Divide sts evenly on 4 needles with 25 sts on each needle. Join, being careful not to twist sts on needles and pm to mark beg of rnd. P2 rnds.

Next rnd With F, knit, inc 2 sts on each of the 4 dpn—108 sts total and 27 sts on each dpn.

Beg chart 1

Rnd 1 Beg with rnd 1 of chart 1, work 12-st rep 9 times around. Cont to foll chart 1 through rnd 36.

Shape top

Beg chart 2

Rnd 1 With MC, knit.

Rnd 2 With MC, work as foll: *Needle 1*, Ssk, k to last 2 sts, k2tog; *Needle 2*, Ssk, k to last 2 sts, k2tog; *Needle 3*, Ssk, k to last 2 sts, k2tog; *Needle 4*, ssk, k to last 2 sts, k2tog—100 sts.

Rnds 3 and 5 Rep rnd 1.

Rnds 4 and 6 Rep rnd 2—84 sts.

Rnds 7 and 8 Foll chart 2, work even with A and B.

Rnds 9, 11 and 13 Rep rnd 1.

Rnds 10, 12 and 14 Rep rnd 2—60 sts.

Rnds 15 and 16 Foll chart 2, work even with C and F.

Rnds 17, 19 and 21 Rep rnd 1.

Rnds 18, 20 and 22 Rep rnd 2-36 sts.

Rnds 23 and 24 Foll chart 2, work even with D and E

Cont rem of cap with MC only.

Rnds 25, 27 and 29 With MC, knit.

Rnds 26, 28 and 30 Rep rnd 2—12 sts .

Rnds 31, 32 and 33 With MC, knit.

Rnd 34 [SK2P] 4 times—4 sts. Cut yarn leaving an end for sewing top.

Pull through rem 4 sts and draw up tightly to secure. Fasten off.

EAR FLAPS

(make 2)

Fold hat in half and mark center 25 sts on one side of cap and center 25 sts on other side of cap.

For first flap, with RS facing and using MC and straight needles, pick up and k 25 sts under the MC rolled edge (that is, pick up sts in the first A row). Working back and forth in rows, p1 row on WS. Then work 4 rows more in St st dec 1 st on last WS row—24 sts.

Beg chart 3

Row 1 (RS) Foll row 1 of chart 3, work 4-st rep 6 times across.

Row 2 Work even foll chart.

Next (dec) row (RS) Cont to foll chart 3, k1, ssk, k to last 3 sts, k2tog, k1.

Next row Cont to foll chart, purl.

Rep last 2 rows, foll chart 3 through row 18, then cont with MC only until 2 sts rem. Bind off 2 sts on last WS row.

Earflap trim

Working from RS at right edge of one earflap, with B, pick up and k22 sts evenly along this edge only to point. K1 row. Bind off knitwise. Then with C, pick up along left edge from point to top and work in same way. Sew trim tog at point.

FINISHING

Block hat flat. Make a 1½"/4cm pompom with E for top of cap. Attach to top of cap.

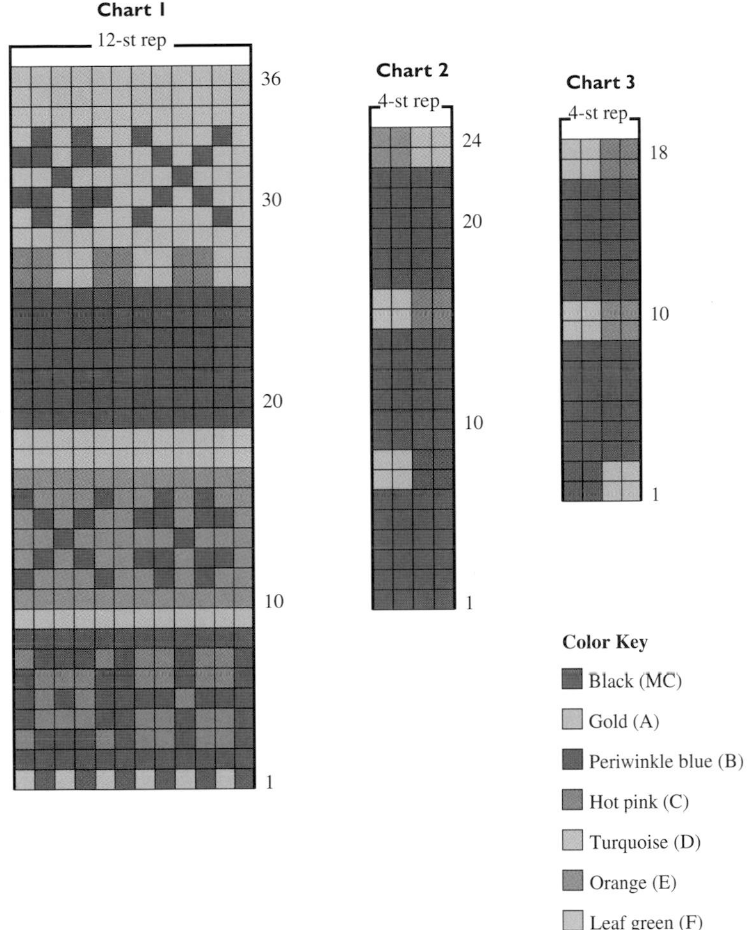
Chart 1
12-st rep
36
30
20
10
1
Chart 2
4-st rep
24
20
10
1
Chart 3
4-st rep
18
10
1
Color Key
Black (MC)
Gold (A)
Periwinkle blue (B)
Hot pink (C)
Turquoise (D)
Orange (E)
Leaf green (F)

BULKY BRIMMED HAT

Fedorable!

For Intermediate Knitters

Based on fabric hat designs constructed in multiple pieces and sewn together, this hat is designed to fit in two different sizes depending on the needle and gauges chosen. Designed by Karen Greenwald.

SIZE

Instructions are written for one size. Change of needle sizes will give a more standard-fitting hat. This hat is a very loose-fitting style.

KNITTED MEASUREMENTS

- Head circumference on (smaller) larger needles 20 (23)"/51 (58.5)cm
- Depth on (smaller) larger needles 7 (8)"/18 (20.5)cm

MATERIALS

- 2 3½oz/100g skeins (each approx 66yd/60m) of Reynolds Bulky *Lopi* (wool ⑥) in #85 oatmeal

For smaller fitting size

- One pair size 10½ (7mm) needles *or size to obtain gauge*
- Size 10½ (7mm) circular needle, 24"/60cm long

For larger fitting size

- One pair size 13 (9mm) needles *or size to obtain gauge*
- Size 13 (9mm) circular needle, 24"/60cm long

GAUGES

For smaller fitting size

- 12 sts and 16 rows to 4"/10cm over St st using size 10½ (7mm) needles.
- 10 sts and 14 rows to 4"/10cm over St st using size 13 (9mm) needles.

Take time to check gauge.

Note Hat is made with one top panel and 2 identical side panels and 2 shorter front panels. Brim is picked up and k after pieces of hat are sewn tog.

SIDES AND TOP PANELS

(make 3)

With chosen needle size, cast on 14 sts for 4½ (5½)"/11.5 (14)cm wide.

Row 1 (RS) Knit.

Row 2 K1, purl to last st, k1.

Rep these 2 rows for St st for 24 rows OR 6 (7)"/15 (18)cm. Bind off.

FRONT AND BACK PANELS

(make 2)

With chosen needle size, cast on 14 sts for 4½ (5½)"/11.5 (14)cm wide.

Row 1 (RS) Knit.

Row 2 K1, purl to last st, k1. Rep these 2 rows for St st for 17 rows OR 4¼ (5)"/11 (12.5)cm. Bind off.

FINISHING

Block pieces to measurements. Lay out pieces so that the cast-on edge of one front panel meets the bound-off edge of one side panel, then the bound-off edge of same front panel meets the cast-on edge of other side panel, then the bound-off edge of same side panel meets the cast-on edge of last front panel. With seams falling to WS, join pieces tog in this order, joining last front panel to first side panel and making piece into a circle. Place top piece at top of hat and working seam from WS so that seam shows on RS (for ridge of hat as shown in photo), weave top of hat to joined sides.

BRIM

Beg at seam on other side of joined hat sides, with chosen size for circular needle, pick up and k 70 sts evenly around lower edge. Join to work in rnds and pm to mark beg of rnd. K 1 rnd.

Next (inc) rnd *K6, inc 1 st in next st; rep from * 9 times more—80 sts. K 1 rnd.

Next (inc) rnd *K7, inc 1 st in next st; rep from * 9 times more—90 sts. P 1 rnd for turning ridge. K 1 rnd.

Next (dec) rnd *K7, k2tog; rep from * 9 times more—80 sts. K 1 rnd.

Next (dec) rnd *K6, k2tog; rep from * 9 times more—70 sts. K 1 rnd. Bind off firmly. Turn brim to WS and tack neatly in place.

FUR-TRIMMED CAP

Going loopy

For Intermediate Knitters

This cap features an attached loop fringe trim that mimics Mongolian lamb. This style was a fashion trend in the 1970's and is popular again today in this design by Lipp Holmfeld.

SIZE

One size fits all. This cap is a loose-fitting style.

KNITTED MEASUREMENTS

- Head circumference 23"/58.5cm
- Depth 8"/20.5cm

MATERIALS

- 1¾oz/50g balls (each approx 153yd/140m) of Anny Blatt *Chimere* (wool/mohair/polyamide ④) in #338 cranberry (A)
- 1¾oz/50g balls (each approx 137yd/125m) of Anny Blatt *Merinos* (wool ④) in #338 fuchsia (B)
- One pair each sizes 9 and 11 (5.5 and 8mm) needles *or size to obtain gauge*

GAUGES

- 17 sts and 26 rows to 4"/10cm over St st using 2 strands B and size 9 (5.5mm) needles.
- 12 sts and 4"/10cm and 5 rows to 2½"/6.5cm needles over loop st pat using 2 strands A and size 11 (8mm) needles.

Take time to check gauges.

LOOP STITCH PATTERN

(odd number of sts)

Row 1 (RS) Knit.

Row 2 Purl.

Row 3 K1, *k1 st in next st only leave the lp that would be dropped on LH needle, [bring yarn around to front of work and wrap yarn clockwise around the left thumb once to make a loop, then bring yarn to back of work and k into the back loop of same st on LH needle for loop st] twice, on the 2nd loop, drop st from LH needle (for 3 sts made in 1 st), k1; rep from * to end.

Row 4 P1, *p3tog, p1; rep from * to end.

Row 5 K2, *make 2 loop sts as on row 3, k1; rep from *, end k1.

Note Work with 2 strands of yarn held together throughout.

CAP

Loop stitch band

Beg at lower edge with 2 strands A and size 11 (8mm) needles, cast on 69 sts. Work in loop st pat for 5 rows. There are 135 sts at end of row 5.

Next row (WS) [P2tog, p1] 4 times, [p2tog, p2] 28 times, [p2tog, p1] 3 times, p2tog—99 sts.

Beg crown

Change to 2 strands B and size 9 (5.5mm) needles. Work in St st for 6 rows.

Next row (RS) K1, *p1, k1; rep from * to end. This row will be the foldline row referred to later under finishing. Then cont in St st for 4"/10cm above foldline, end with a WS row.

Shape crown

Next row (RS) K1, [k2tog, k5] 14 times—85 sts. Work 3 rows even.

Next row K1, [k2tog, k4] 14 times—71 sts. Work 3 rows even.

Next row K1, [k2tog, k3] 14 times—57 sts. Work 1 row even.

Next row K1, [k2tog, k2] 14 times—43 sts. Work 1 row even.

Next row K1, [k2tog, k1] 4 times—29 sts. Work 1 row even.

Next row K1, [k2tog] 14 times—15 sts. Work 1 row even.

Next row K1, [k2tog] 7 times—8 sts. Cut yarn leaving a long end for sewing and pull through rem 8 sts. Draw up tightly to secure.

FINISHING

Sew back seam. Block lightly. Fold cap along foldline (so there is a 1"/2.5cm overlap in B yarn at lower edge) and with single strand B, tack loop st back through both thicknesses of lower edge.

POMPOM

Wrap 2 strands of A around fingers to desired thickness. Cut yarn, tie around center of loops and knot. Pull loops apart to neaten and sew to top of hat.

SEED STITCH BABY CAP

Flower power

Simple seed stitch is worked straight, then decreased along the crown in nine easy rows, making this cap a perfect beginner's project. Designed by Jean Guirguis in soft cotton and acrylic yarn, perfect for a delicate little head.

SIZES

Instructions are written for size Infant's size 6-12 months. Changes for size 24 months are in parentheses. Shown in size 6-12 months. This cap is a standard-fitting style.

KNITTED MEASUREMENTS

- Head circumference 17 (18)"/43 (45.5)cm
- Depth (with edge rolled) 5½"/14cm

MATERIALS

- 1 3½oz/100g ball (each approx 135yd/124m) of Reynolds/JCA *Cabana* (cotton/acrylic ⑤) in #960 rose
- One pair size 7 (4.5mm) needles *or size to obtain gauge*
- Purchased silk flowers (optional)

GAUGE

16 sts and 24 rows to 4"/10cm over seed st using size 7 (4.5mm) needles.

Take time to check gauge.

SEED STITCH PATTERN

(over an even number of sts)

Row 1 (RS) *K1, p1; rep from * to end.

Row 2 *P1, kl; rep from * to end.

Rep these 2 rows for pat (that is, always k the purl sts and p the knit sts).

CAP

Beg at lower edge with size 7 (4.5mm) needles, cast on 68 (72) sts. Work in seed st for 2"/5cm. Work even until piece measures 6 (6½)"/15 (16.5)cm from beg.

Shape crown

Row 1 Work 5 (7) sts in seed st, *SK2P, work 8 sts in seed st; rep from * 4 times more, SK2P, work 5 (7) sts in seed st—56 (60) sts.

Row 2 Work even in seed st.

Row 3 Work 4 (6) sts in seed st, *SK2P, work 6 sts in seed st; rep from * 4 times more, SK2P, work 4 (6) sts in seed st—44 (48) sts.

Row 4 Work even in seed st.

Row 5 Work 3 (5) sts in seed st, *SK2P, work 4 sts in seed st; rep from * 4 times more, SK2P, work 3 (5) sts in seed st—32 (36) sts.

Row 6 Work even in seed st.

Row 7 Work 2 (4) sts in seed st, *SK2P, work 2 sts in seed st; rep from * 4 times more, SK2P, work 2 (4) sts in seed st 20 (24) sts.

Row 8 Work even in seed st.

Row 9 K1 (0), [SK2P] 6 (8) times, k1 (0)—8 sts. Cut yarn leaving a long length for sewing seam and tacking brim. Pull through rem 8 sts and draw up tightly to secure.

FINISHING

Block lightly to measurements. Sew back seam to last 2"/5cm at brim. Roll brim so that 1"/2.5cm is doubled and sew seam so that seam is on inside. Cont to tack rolled brim in place from WS. Attach silk flowers if desired.

RIBBED BANDED CAP

Cable hook-up

An easy rib-style cap knit in sumptuous mohair yarn gets an adjustable cable trim that fastens in the back seam for a snug fit. Designed by Irina Poludnenko.

SIZES

One size fits all.

KNITTED MEASUREMENTS

- Head circumference 21"/53cm
- Depth 8½"/21.5cm

MATERIALS

- 3 .88oz/25g balls (each approx 149yd/138m) of GGH Muench Yarns *Soft Kid* (mohair/polyamide/wool ②) in #53 purple
- One pair size 7 (4.5mm) needles *or size to obtain gauge*
- Cable needle (cn)

GAUGE

17 sts and 22 rows to 4"/10cm over k3, p2 rib (slightly stretched) using 2 strands of yarn and size 7 (4.5mm) needles.
Take time to check gauge.

Note Work with 2 strands of yarn held together throughout.

CAP

Beg at lower edge with 2 strands of yarn and size 7 (4.5mm) needles, cast on 92 sts.
Row 1 (RS) K1 (selvage st), *k3, p2; rep from *, end k1 (selvage st).
Row 2 K1, *k2, p3; rep from *, end k1.
Rep these 2 rows for k3, p2 rib until piece measures 7½"/19cm from beg.

Shape top

Row 1 (RS) K1, *k2tog, k1, p2; rep from *, end k1 —74 sts.
Row 2 Work in k2, p2 rib as established.
Row 3 K1, *k2tog, p2; rep from *, end k1 —56 sts.
Row 4 K1, *k2, p1; rep from *, end k1.
Row 5 K1, *k1, p2tog; rep from *, end k1 —38 sts.
Row 6 Work in k1, p1 rib as established.
Row 7 K1, [k2tog] 18 times, k1 —20 sts.
Row 8 Purl. Cut yarn, leaving long end for sewing. Pull through rem sts on needle and draw up tightly and secure. Fasten off but leave end for seaming with band later.

BAND

With 2 strands of yarn and size 7 (4.5mm) needles, cast on 20 sts.

Row 1 (RS) Knit.
Rows 2, 4, 6 and 8 Purl.

Row 3 K1, *sl next 3 sts to cn and hold to *back*, k3, k3 from cn, k3; rep from * once more, k1.

Row 5 Knit.

Row 7 K1, *k3, sl next 3 sts to cn and hold to *front*, k3, k3 from cn; rep from * once more, k1.

Rep rows 1-8 for 21"/53cm. Bind off.

FINISHING

Block lightly to measurements. Pin cable band to lower edge of hat at ½"/1.5cm from lower edge. Sew back seam along with band, in place.

MULTICOLOR FUNNEL HAT

Twist and tie

For Intermediate Knitters

Multicolor pattern bands on this hat are separated with colorful garter ridges and trimmed at the lower edge with a bi-colored rib. Designed by Svetlana Avrakk, the funnel style is closed with a two-color twisted rope tie.

SIZE

One size fits all. This cap is a loose-fitting style.

KNITTED MEASUREMENTS

- Head circumference 20½"/52cm
- Depth (excluding cinched top) 10"/25.5cm

MATERIALS

- 1 3½oz/100g ball (each approx 223yd/204m) of Patons® *Classic Merino Wool* (wool ③) each in #238 orange (MC), #204 gold (A), #213 blue (B), #240 green (C) and #207 red (D)
- One pair each sizes 6 and 7 (4 and 4.5mm) needles *or size to obtain gauge*

GAUGE

22 sts and 26 rows to 4"/10cm over St st foll charts using larger needles.

Take time to check gauge.

Note When changing colors, bring new yarn from underneath working yarn to avoid holes in work.

HAT

Beg at lower edge with smaller needles and MC, cast on 106 sts.

Row 1 (WS) Knit.

Row 2 With A, k2, * with B, k2, with A, k2; rep from * to end.

Row 3 With A, p2, * with B, k2, with A, p2; rep from * to end.

Row 4 With A, k2, *with B, p2, with A, k2; rep from * to end.

Rep rows 3 and 4 for 2-color rib once more. Then rep row 3 once. Change to larger needles. With C, k1 row, p1 row. With B, k2 rows. With C, k1 row.

Next row (WS) With C, purl, inc 6 sts evenly spaced across—112 sts.

Beg chart 1

Row 1 (RS) Foll row 1 of chart 1, work 8-st rep 14 times across. Cont to foll chart 1 through row 15.

Next row (WS) With C, purl, dec 6 sts evenly spaced across—106 sts. With C, k1 row, p1 row. With D, k2 rows.

Beg chart 2

Row 1 (RS) Beg with st 1 of row 1, work to end of row, then work 4-st rep across row 25 times more. Cont to foll chart 2 through row 5. With C, p2 rows.

Beg chart 3

Row 1 (WS) With MC, foll row 1 of chart 3, purl. Cont to foll chart 3, purl. Cont to foll chart 3, working rows 2-5 and working 2-st rep across. With A, k2 rows.

Beg chart 4

Row 1 (RS) Beg with st 1 of row 1, work even with C across. Cont to foll chart 4, working 2-st rep 53 times across, through row 10.

Shape top

Row 1 (RS) With MC, k3, [k2tog, k8] 10 times, k3—96 sts.

Row 2 With MC, knit.

Row 3 With C, k3, [k2tog, k7] 10 times, k3—86 sts.

Row 4 With C, purl.

Row 5 With B, k3, [k2tog, k6] 10 times, k3—76 sts.

Row 6 With B, purl.

Row 7 With D, k3, [k2tog, k5] 10 times, k3—66 sts.

Row 8 With D, knit.

Row 9 With C, k3, [k2tog, k4] 10 times, k3—56 sts.

Row 10 With A, purl.

Row 11 With A, k3, [k2tog, k3] 10 times, k3—46 sts.

With A, [p1 row, k1 row] twice. With B, [k1 row, p1 row] 3 times.

Beg chart 5

Row 1 (RS) Work 2-st rep of row 1 of chart 5 23 times across. Work row 2 of chart 5. With C, knit 1 row. With C, bind off knitwise on WS, leaving a long end for sewing back seam.

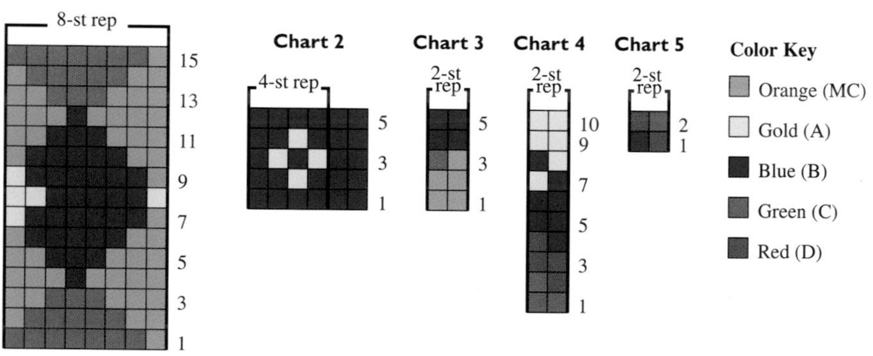

FINISHING

Sew back seam. Block hat flat.

Twisted cord

Cut 6 strands A and 5 strands D each 20"/51cm long. Using the 2 colors, make a twisted cord by holding one set of ends by one person and the other set of ends by another person. Each person should twist the ends to their right until the cord begins to curl. The cord will twist around itself. Knot both ends. Tie cord around top of hat around the A color band as shown in photo.

HORSESHOE CABLE CAP

Pretty in pink

A traditional cable pattern gives depth to this simple fitted cap. Knits up fast using two strands of yarn, this design is by Mickey Landau.

SIZE

One size fits all. This cap is a standard-fitting style.

KNITTED MEASUREMENTS

- Head circumference 21"/53cm
- Depth 8¼"/21cm

MATERIALS

- 2 3½oz/100g balls (each approx 211yd/95m) of Colorado Yarns *Knitaly* (wool ④) in #1912 pink
- Size 10½ (7mm) circular needle, 16"/40cm long *or size to obtain gauge*
- One set (5) size 10½ (7mm) dpn
- Cable needle (cn)

GAUGE

16 sts and 20 rows to 4"/10cm over St st using 2 strands of yarn and size 10½ (7mm) needles.

Take time to check gauge.

HORSESHOE CABLE PATTERN

(multiple of 16 sts and worked in rnds)

Rnds 1, 2 and 3 *K12, p4; rep from * around.

Rnd 4 *Sl 3 sts to cn and hold to *back*, k3, k3 from cn, sl next 3 sts to cn and hold to *front*, k3, k3 from cn, p4; rep from * around.

Rep rnds 1-4 for horseshoe cable pat.

Note Work with 2 strands of yarn held together throughout.

CAP

Beg at lower edge with circular needle and 2 strands of yarn, cast on 96 sts. Join to work in rnds. Pm at beg of rnd. Work in k1, p1 rib for 2"/5cm. Then work in horseshoe cable pat for 3"/7.5cm.

Dec rnd *Work 12 sts, p1, p2tog, p1; rep from * around—90 sts. Work even for 3 rnds.

Dec rnd *Work 12 sts, p1, p2tog; rep from * around—84 sts. Work even for 3 rnds.

Dec rnd *Work 12 sts, p2tog; rep from * around—78 sts. Change to dpn to accommodate fewer sts.

Next rnd *[K2tog] 6 times, p1; rep from * around—42 sts.

Next rnd *[K2tog] 3 times, p1; rep from * around—24 sts.

Next rnd *K2tog, sl 1, p1, psso; rep from * around—12 sts. Cut yarn leaving a

12"/30.5 length. Pull yarn through rem sts and draw up tightly to secure.

FINISHING

I-cord

With 2 dpn, cast on 3 sts. *K3, do not turn. Slide sts to beg of needle and bring yarn around from back to k3 from same position again. Rep from * for I-cord for 6"/15cm. Bind off.

Tassel

Wind yarn 42 times around a 4½"/11.5cm cardboard. Pull strand of yarn through lps at top and tie tightly to fasten. Cut other end of yarn at opposite side of cardboard. Wind yarn around top of tassel at 1"/2.5cm from top. Fasten to end of I-cord. Fasten other end of I-cord to top of cap.

BABY'S EARFLAP CAPS

Take two

These simple hats are knit flat with easy top shaping, two-color striped earflaps, and an easy crochet edge. Designed by Veronica Manno.

SIZE

One size fits infant's 6-12 months. This cap is a loose-fitting style.

FINISHED MEASUREMENTS

- Head circumference 17"/43cm
- Depth (excluding earflaps) 5½"/14cm

MATERIALS

- 1 ball each (each approx 105yd/96m) of Cleckheaton/Plymouth Yarns *Country 8-Ply* (wool ④) in #2232 red (A) and #2231 coral (B), OR #1860 purple (A) and #2230 aqua (B)
- One pair size 6 (4mm) needles *or size to obtain gauge*
- Size G/6 (4.5mm) crochet hook
- Stitch markers

GAUGE

19 sts and 28 rows to 4"/10cm over St st using size 6 (4mm) needles.
Take time to check gauge.

CAP

Beg at lower edge with A, cast on 80 sts. Work in St st for 5"/12.5cm.

Top shaping

Next row (RS) *K6, k2tog; rep from * to end—70 sts.
Next row Purl.
Next row *K5, k2tog; rep from * to end—60 sts.
Next row Purl.
Next row *K4, k2tog, rep from * to end—50 sts.
Next row Purl.
Next row *K3, k2tog; rep from * to end—40 sts.
Next row Purl.
Next row *K2, k2tog; rep from * to end—30 sts.
Next row Purl.
Next row *K1, k2tog; rep from * to end—20 sts.
Next row Purl.
Next row *K2tog; rep from * to end—10 sts.
Cut yarn leaving long end for sewing seam and pull through rem sts and draw up tightly to secure. Sew back seam and fasten off.

FINISHING

Block cap flat.

EARFLAPS

Place 2 markers either side of center front

20 sts of cap. Pm at 18 sts to the left and 18 sts to the right of these 2 markers. Working from RS, with B, pick up and k one set of 18 sts for one earflap.

Row 1 (WS) With B, purl.

Row 2 (RS) With B, knit, dec 1 st each side of row—16 sts.

Row 3 With B, purl.

Row 4 With A, knit, dec 1 st each side of row—14 sts.

Rows 5 and 7 With A, purl.

Row 6 With A, knit.

Row 8 With B, knit, dec 1 st each side of row—12 sts.

Rows 9 and 11 With B, purl.

Row 10 With B, knit, dec 1 st each side of row—10 sts.

Row 12 With A, knit, dec 1 st each side of row—8 sts

Row 13 With A, purl.

Row 14 With A, knit, dec 1 st each side of row—6 sts. On next WS row, bind off 6 sts. Work other earflap in same way.

With crochet hook and B, join with a sl st and beg at center back seam, *work 1 sc in each st along lower edge, 11 sts along side of one earflap, 6 sts across lower edge of earflap, 11 sts along other side of earflap; rep from * once, work 1 sc in each sc to end. Join with a sl st to first sc and fasten off.

TWISTED CORDS

(make 2)

Cut 1 strand each of A and B 30"/76cm long. Make a twisted cord and attach with a knot pulled through from WS at sc edge.

Pompom

Make a 2"/5cm pompom. Trim pompom and fasten to top of cap.

CAP WITH BRAIDED TRIM

Alpine Miss

For Experienced Knitters

North Country winter pastels and refined details are the unique elements that make up this helmet styled cap. Fine two-color braid knitting and chunky cord complete this hat design by Svetlana Avrakk.

SIZE

One size fits all. This cap is a standard-fitting style.

KNITTED MEASUREMENTS

- Head circumference 20"/51cm
- Depth (excluding earflaps) 8½"/21.5cm

MATERIALS

- 2 1¾oz/50g balls (each approx 203yd/186m) of Patons® *Kroy* (wool/nylon ①) in #54048 silver grey (MC)
- 1 ball each in #54044 med grey (A), #54008 cream (B) and #54107 blue (C)
- One pair size 2 (2.75mm) needles *or size to obtain gauge*
- One set (5) size 2 (2.75mm) dpn

GAUGE

30 sts and 39 rows to 4"/10cm over St st foll chart using size 2 (2.75mm) needle.
Take time to check gauge.

Note When changing colors foll chart, bring new yarn from underneath working yarn to avoid holes in work.

First Earflap

Using straight needles, with MC, cast on 18 sts.

Row 1 (RS) Inc 1 st in first st, k to last 2 sts, inc 1 st in next st, k1.

Row 2 Purl.

Rep last 2 rows 4 times more—28 sts.

Next row Rep row 1—30 sts.

Work 3 rows even.

Rep last 4 rows once more—32 sts. Cut yarn and leave sts on spare needle.

Second Earflap

Work as for first earflap, only do not cut MC at end of working.

CAP

Joining row (RS)

With MC, cast on 17 sts, k32 sts from second earflap, turn. Cast on 52 sts, turn.

Next row Cont with MC, k32 sts of first earflap, turn. Cast on 17 sts—150 sts. Turn and working in rnds from this point on 4 dpn, join sts and pm to mark beg of rnd. Divide sts so there are 37 sts on 2 needles and 38 sts on 2 needles. With MC, k6 rnds

** **Next rnd** *With B, k1, with MC, k1, rep from * around.

Next (braided) rnd Working with both strands of yarn in front of work across the entire rnd, work as foll: *Bringing the next color to purl over the last st worked (this will twist the yarn as you purl around), with B, p1, with MC, p1; rep from * around.

Next (braided) rnd Working with both strands of yarn in front of work across the entire rnd, *bringing the next color to purl under the last st (this untwists the yarn as you purl around), with B, p1, with MC, p1; rep from * around **.

+Rep between **'s once, only substitute MC for B and A for MC. Rep between **'s once using colors as described +. With A, k6 rnds.

Rep between +'s once.

Next rnd With MC, *k7, inc 1 st in the next st; rep from * 17 times more—168 sts.

Beg chart 1

Rnd 1 Working rnd 1 of chart 1, work 24-st rep 7 times around. Cont to foll chart 1 through rnd 25.

Next rnd With MC, *k12, k2tog; rep from * 11 times more—156 sts.

Next rnd *With MC, k1, with A, k1; rep from * around.

Next (braided) rnd Working with both strands of yarn in front of work across entire rnd, work as foll: * bringing the next color to purl over the last st worked (this will twist the yarn as you purl around), with MC, p1, with A, p1; rep from * around.

Next rnd With MC, knit.

Shape top

Beg chart 2

Rnd 1 *With MC, k1, SKP, work rnd 1 of chart 2 across next 33 sts, with MC, k2tog, k1; rep from * 3 times more.

Rnd 2 *With MC, k2, work rnd 2 of chart 2 across next 33 sts, with MC, k2; rep from * 3 times more.

Rnd 3 *With MC, k1, SKP, work rnd 3 of chart 2 across next 31 sts, with MC, k2tog, k1; rep from * 3 times more.

Rnd 4 *With MC, k2, work rnd 4 of chart 2 across next 31 sts, with MC, k2; rep from * 3 times more. Cont to work chart 2 in this way, dec 8 sts in MC every alternate rnd as established until chart 2 is completed and 20 sts rem. Cut yarn leaving end for sewing top. Pull through rem 20 sts on needles and draw up tightly to secure. Fasten off.

FINISHING

Block flat to measurements.

Lower edge trim

Beg at the center back of cap, with RS facing, A and 4 dpn, pick up and k sts as foll: 17 sts from lower back cast-on edge, 13 sts along shaped edge of first earflap, 18 sts along cast-on edge of earflap, 13 sts along other shaped edge of earflap, 52 sts from first cast-on edge, 13 sts along shaped edge of second earflap, 18 sts along cast-on edge of earflap, 13 sts along other shaped edge of earflap, 17 sts from lower back cast-on edge—174 sts. Join and work in rnds. Pm to mark beg of rnd.

Next rnd *With A, k1, with B, k1; rep from * around.

Next (braided) rnd Working with both strands of yarn in front of work across the entire rnd, work as foll: *bringing the next color to purl over the last st worked (this will twist the yarn as you purl around), with A, p1, with B, p1; rep from * around. With A, k8 rnds. Bind off. Fold edging along braided rnd to WS and sew in place.

Braid

Cut 26 strands each of colors MC, A and B at 14"/36cm long. Make a braid as shown, wrapping MC around ends. Attach to top of cap.

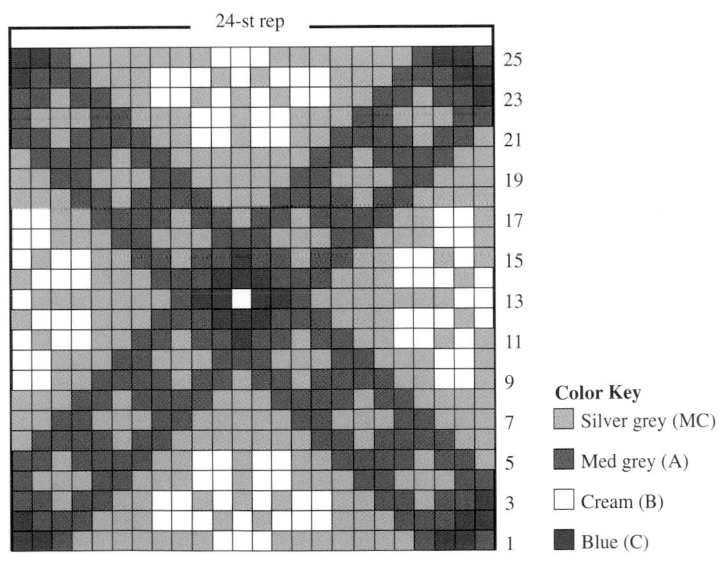

Chart 2

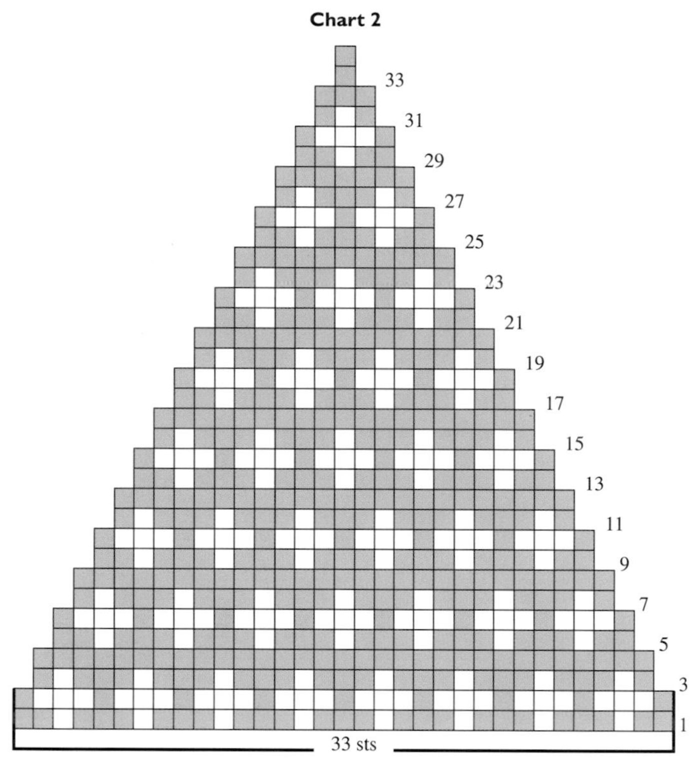

Color Key

- Silver grey (MC)
- Med grey (A)
- Cream (B)
- Blue (C)

STRIPED HAT

Four corners

For Beginner Knitters

Use your yarn scraps in shades of blue and green, or five favorite shades, to make this super easy garter stitch cap for little ones. This design by Nicky Epstein is trimmed on the four points with tiny bobbles.

SIZE

One size fits Baby/Toddler's size. This cap is a standard-fitting style.

KNITTED MEASUREMENTS

- Head circumference 18"/45.5cm
- Depth 5"/12.5cm

MATERIALS

Note Use small amounts of the foll colors, (or 1 skein each):

- 1 3½oz/100g skein each (each approx 215yd/197m) of Brown Sheep Yarn Co. *Cotton Fleece* (cotton/wool ④) in #590 lapis (A), # 840 lime (B), #560 lt blue (C), #765 turquoise (D) and #870 mint (E)
- One pair size 5 (3.75mm) needles *or size to obtain gauge*

GAUGE

20 sts and 40 rows to 4"/10cm over garter st using size 5 (3.75mm) needles.

Take time to check gauge.

Note When working stripe pat, do not cut yarns when changing colors. Carry yarns along side of rows and twist tog every few rows to avoid sewing in ends later.

CAP

Beg at lower edge with A, cast on 90 sts, leaving a long end for sewing back seam. K1 row.

Row 2 (RS) With B, k3, sl 1 st purlwise, *k5, sl 1 purlwise; rep from *, end k2.

Row 3 (WS) With B, k2, sl 1 st purlwise with yarn in front of work, *k5, sl 1 st purlwise with yarn in front of work; rep from *, end k3. Rep rows 2 and 3 twice more. Then cont in garter st and stripe pat as foll: 2 rows C, 2 rows E, 2 rows D, 2 rows A, 2 rows B, 2 rows E, 2 rows C, 2 rows A, 2 rows D, 4 rows B, 2 rows E, 4 rows A, 2 rows D, 6 rows C, 2 rows E, 2 rows A, 2 rows B, 2 rows D. Piece measures approx 5¼"/13.5cm from beg. Place contrast yarn markers at the foll 4 intervals: st 12 (marker 1), st 34 (marker 2), st 56 (marker 3) and st 78 (marker 4). Leave markers in and bind off all sts (be sure not to bind off too tightly).

FINISHING

Block lightly, sew back seam. Fold hat at bound-off edges in half and seam along bound-off edges. With RS facing, make a vertical foldline at marker 1 and marker 2 and determine middle point between these markers and place pin here; make a similar vertical foldline at marker 3 and marker 4 and place pin at middle point between these 2 markers. Then line up pins to match at top center of hat and tack center top tog through 4 sts at center top hat. The four points are now formed, one point at top of each foldline. Press lightly to define the 4 foldlines.

Bobbles

(make 12 in varying colors)

With chosen color, cast on 1 st. K1 st into front, back, front, back and front of st for 5 sts. P1 row, k1 row, p1 row. K2tog, k1, k2tog, turn. P3tog. Fasten off. Sew a cluster of 3 bobbles to top of each of the 4 corners.

KID'S COTTON CAP

Feeling sheepish?

For Intermediate Knitters

Little wooly sheep are stitched to resemble fleece in this easy cap topped with simple stripes. Designed by Amy Bahrt with a chain stitch bow tied at the crown.

SIZE

Instructions are written for one size, Infant's one year. This cap is a standard-fitting size.

KNITTED MEASUREMENTS

- Head circumference 17½"/44.5cm
- Depth 6¼"/16cm

MATERIALS

- 1 1¾oz/50g ball (each approx 105yd/95m) of Tahki Yarn/Tahki•Stacy Charles, Inc. *Cotton Classic II* (cotton ④) each in #2847 lt blue (MC), #2039 charcoal (A) and #2001 white (B)
- One pair each sizes 5 and 7 (3.75 and 4.5mm) needles *or size to obtain gauge*
- Size E/4 (3.5mm) crochet hook
- Tapestry needle

GAUGE

18 sts and 24 rows to 4"/10cm over St st using larger needles.

Take time to check gauge.

Note Work each chart motif with a separate ball or bobbin of color. Do not carry yarns across back of work between motifs.

CAP

Beg at lower edge with smaller needles and MC, cast on 79 sts. Work in k1, p1 rib for 1"/2.5cm.

Beg chart pat

Row 1 (RS) With MC, k7, *work 12 sts of chart pat, with MC, k6; rep from * 3 times. Cont to foll chart in this way through row 12. Then with MC, work in St st for 4 rows more.

Shape top

Row 1 (RS) With B, *k9, k2tog; rep from * 6 times more, k2—72 sts.

Row 2 With B, purl.

Row 3 With MC, *k8, k2tog; rep from * 6 times more, k2—65 sts.

Row 4 With MC, purl.

Row 5 With MC, *k7, k2tog; rep from * 6 times more, k2—58 sts.

Row 6 With MC, purl.

Row 7 With B, *k6, k2tog; rep from * 6 times more, k2—51 sts.

Row 8 With B, purl.

Row 9 With MC, *k5, k2tog; rep from * 6 times more, k2—44 sts.

Row 10 With MC, purl.

Row 11 With MC, *k4, k2tog; rep from * 6 times more, k2—37 sts.

Row 12 With MC, purl.

Row 13 With B, *k3, k2tog; rep from *, end k2—30 sts.
Row 14 With B, purl.
Row 15 With B, [k2tog] 15 times—15 sts. Cut yarn leaving long end for sewing and pull through rem sts and draw up tightly to secure. Sew back seam.

FINISHING

Block cap flat. With B, using tapestry needle, work ch-st loop for ear (see chart) on each sheep motif.

TIE

With crochet hook and B, ch for 13"/ 33cm. Leaving a ½"/1.5cm end at each end of tie, trim ends of chain tie. Tie chain into a bow and fasten securely at top of cap.

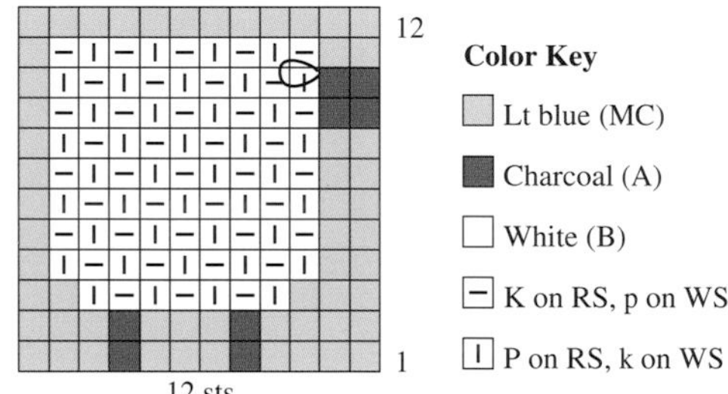

FAIR ISLE SKI CAP

Powder power

For Intermediate Knitters

This ski cap is fit for men or women and is completely devoid of the shaping most commonly used in the crown section. Ribbed band under the turnback ensures a snug fit in this cap design by Jean Guirguis.

SIZES

Instructions are written for Man's/ Woman's size Small (21"/53cm). Changes for sizes Medium (22"/56cm) and Large (23"/59cm) are in parentheses. Shown in size Small. This cap is a close-fitting style.

KNITTED MEASUREMENTS

- Head circumference 18½ (19½, 20½)"/47 (49.5, 52)cm
- Depth (with folded cuff) 8"/20.5cm

MATERIALS

- 2 1¾oz/50g balls (each approx 148yd/136m) of Dale of Norway *Sisik* (acrylic/wool/mohair/rayon ②) in #160 brown tweed (A)
- 1 ball in #1023 camel tweed (B)
- One pair size 4 (3.5mm) needles *or size to obtain gauge*

GAUGE

26 sts and 30 rows to 4"/10cm over St st foll charts using size 4 (3.5mm) needles. *Take time to check gauge.*

Note When changing colors, bring working yarn from under previous color for jacquard knitting technique.

CAP

Beg at lower edge with size 4 (3.5mm) needles and A, cast on 120 (126, 134) sts. Work in k1, p1 rib for 4 rows.

Beg chart I

Row I (RS) Beg with st 1, work 4 st rep 29 (30, 32) times, work sts 5 to 8 (10, 10). Cont to foll chart 1 through row 21. Change to A only and work in k1, p1 rib for 3"/7.5cm, end with a RS row.

Note The next row to beg chart 2 will be a RS row of chart to reverse the direction of the chart for the cuff turnback.

Beg chart 2

Row I (RS) Beg with st 1, work 6-st rep across row, ending with st 6 (6, 8). Cont to foll chart 2, rep rows 1-16 for a total of 6"/15cm in chart 2 pat. Cut yarn leaving a long end for drawing through all sts on needle and sewing back seam.

FINISHING

Block lightly, do not press or flatten ribbing. Pull double strands of yarn through all 120 (126, 134) sts on needle, gather top and draw up tightly and secure. Sew back seam, sewing cuff seam to that seam is on WS for cuff foldback.

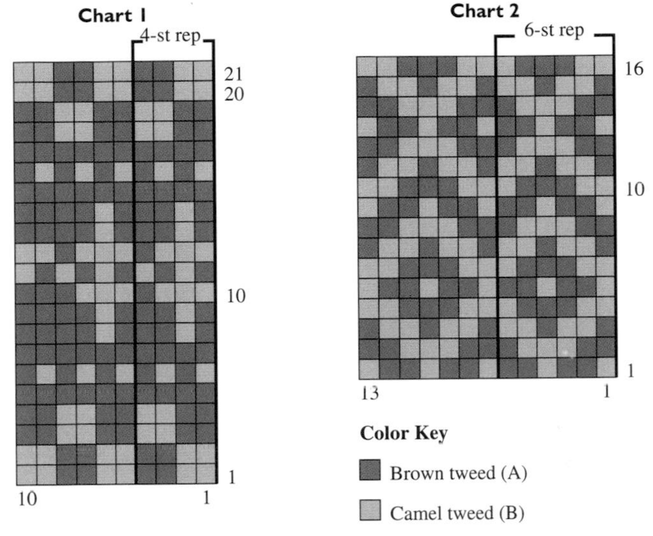
Chart 1
4-st rep
21
20
10
1
10
1
Chart 2
6-st rep
16
10
1
13
1
Color Key
Brown tweed (A)
Camel tweed (B)

DANCING BEARS CAP

Teddy bears on parade

For Experienced Knitters

Dimensional teddy bears are knit into this whimsical hat and form the trim on the ties for a one-of-a-kind child's cap style. Designed by Barbara Telford in sturdy wool tweed yarn.

SIZES

Instructions are written for Infant's one-year size. Changes for Toddler's two-year size are in parentheses. This cap is a standard-fitting style.

KNITTED MEASUREMENTS

- Head circumference 17 (18½)"/43 (47)cm
- Depth (excluding earflaps) 6¼ (6½)"/16 (16.5)cm

MATERIALS

- 1 4oz/125g skein (each approx 272yd/251m) of Briggs and Little *Regal Yarn* (wool ③) each in med blue tweed (MC), red tweed (A), pink tweed (B), brown tweed (C), lt blue tweed (D) and natural tweed (E)
- One set (5) each sizes 4 and 7 (3.5 and 4.5mm) dpn *or size to obtain gauge*
- Size F/5 (4mm) crochet hook

GAUGE

19 sts and 24 rows/rnds to 4"/10cm over St st foll chart using size 7 (4.5mm) needles. *Take time to check gauge.*

CAP

Earflaps

(make 2)

With MC and 2 size 7 (4.5mm) dpn, cast on 3 sts.

***Next row** K3, slide sts to beg of needle to knit same sts from RS. Bring yarn around from back to beg of needle. Rep from * for I-cord for 6"/15cm.

Row 1 K1, M1, k1, M1, k1.

Row 2 Purl.

Row 3 K2, M1, k1, M1, k2.

Row 4 Purl.

Row 5 K2, M1, k to last 2 sts, M1, k2.

Rep last 2 rows 7 times more—23 sts.

Purl next row and place on spare needle.

CAP

With size 7 (4.5mm) dpn and MC, cast on 80 (88) sts. Join taking care not to twist sts on needles and divide sts on 3 needles with 26 (28) sts on needle 1, 26 (32) sts on needle 2 and 28 sts on needle 3. Pm to mark beg of rnds. K4 rnds.

Join earflaps

Next rnd K5 sts, place flap behind the cap sts with RS facing RS of cap and *[k1 st of cap tog with 1 st of earlflap] 23 times*, k24 (32) sts of cap; rep between *'s once, k5 sts of cap. K4 rnds.

Beg chart

Rnd 1 Work rnd 1 of chart working 4-st rep 20 (22) times around. Cont to foll chart through rnd 4. Then foll rnds 5-21 of chart, work 10 (11) st rep 8 times around. Then foll rnds 22-25 of chart, work 4-st rep 20 (22) times around. Then with MC, k1 (3) rnds. Cont with MC only to end of cap.

Shape top

Rnd 1 [K6, k2tog] 10 (11) times—70 (77) sts.

Rnd 2 and all even rnds Knit.

Rnd 3 [K5, k2tog] 10 (11) times—60 (66) sts.

Rnd 5 [K4, k2tog] 10 (11) times—50 (55) sts.

Rnd 7 [K3, k2tog] 10 (11) times—40 (44) sts.

Rnd 9 [K2, k2tog] 10 (11) times—30 (33) sts.

Rnd 11 [K1, k2tog] 10 (11) times—20 (22) sts.

Rnd 13 [K2tog] 10 (11) times—10 (11) sts.

Rnd 14 Knit. Cut yarn and pull through rem 10 (11) sts and draw up tightly to secure.

FINISHING

Block lightly to measurements with lower edge rolled (do not press this edge flat).

DIMENSIONAL TEDDY BEARS

(make 5)

Note These teddy bears are worked separately and attached to 3 top chains and 2 I-cords at ends of earflaps.

Beg at top of bear with two size 4 (3.5mm) dpn and C, cast on 3 sts.

Row 1 Knit.

Row 2 *Purl front and back and front of st for 3 sts in 1 st; rep from * twice more—9 sts.

Row 3 K3, then make ear bobble in next st as foll: k1 into front, back and front of st, turn, p3, turn, k3, turn; p3, turn. K3tog tbl; then with LH needle, pick up st in row below this st and knit this st, pass bobble made st over this st (ear completed), k1, work ear bobble in next st, k3.

Row 4 Purl.

Row 5 With C, k4, then with B, work nose bobble as on chart (see chart for explanation), with C, k4.

Row 6 Purl.

Row 7 K4, k1 into front, back and front of st, k4—11 sts.

Row 8 P5 with C, p1 with E, p5 with C.

Row 9 K4 with C, k3 with E, k4 with C.

Row 10 P3 with C, p5 with E, p3 with C.

Row 11 Rep row 9.

Row 12 Rep row 8.

Row 13 With C, knit.

Row 14 With C, purl.

Beg legs

Row 15 K4, k2tog, turn. Work on these 5 sts for first leg for 3 rows in St st.

Next row P5tog. Cut yarn and draw through rem st. Work 2nd leg on rem 5 sts in same way.

Arms

Locate the C st at 3 sts to the left and 3 sts to the right of center E st on row 8. This will be the placement of the 2 arms in C. With a 12"/31cm piece of C yarn folded in half, with crochet hook, ch 5 and join to body at determined placement. Secure in place and make other arm in same way. Stuffing bear with yarn pieces, sew back, leg and crotch seams of bears.

Bow ties

(in alternating A and B colors)

Making one bow tie for each teddy bear on

cap and at I-cord ends, with crochet hook, ch 28. Tie chain into bow tie and fasten to each teddy bear on cap (see photo for alternating colors). Tie bow ties around neck of each dimensional teddy bear.

Teddy bear legs

For teddy bear legs on the cap (there are 8 teddy bears around cap), work 2 I-cords for each bear as foll: For each leg, with smaller dpn and C, cast on 4 sts, work in 4-st I-cord for 5 rows. Hold leg at front of work and picking up 2 sts on row 10 of teddy bear chart, *k2 sts from dpn tog with 1 picked-up st on teddy bear; rep from * once more. Join 2nd leg to last 2 sts of teddy bear chart on row 10.

To complete cap, for top of cap make three 4-st I-cords each 2¼"/6cm long, using MC and size 4 (3.5mm) dpn. Attach 1 teddy bear to each I-cord, pin I-cords to top of cap.

4-st rep

25

23

21

19

17

15

13

11

9

7

5

3

1

4-st rep

10-st rep Infant's

11-st rep Toddler's

Color Key

- Red tweed (A)
- Pink tweed (B)
- Brown tweed (C)
- Lt blue tweed (D)
- Natural tweed (E)
- • *Nose bobble in natural tweed (E)

*to make bobble, with E, k1 into front, back, front and back of st, turn: p4, turn; k4togtbl. Then with LH needle, pick up st in row below and k this st with C pass E st over this st.

RESOURCES

US RESOURCES

Write to the yarn companies listed below for purchasing and mail-order information.

ANNY BLATT
7796 Boardwalk
Brighton, MI 48116

ARTFUL YARNS
distributed by
JCA

AURORA YARN
P.O. Box 3068
Moss Beach, CA 94038

BERGERE DE FRANCE
distributed by
Skacel Collection, Inc.

BRIGGS LITTLE
distributed by
Schoolhouse Press

BROWN SHEEP CO.
100662 County Road 16
Mitchell, NE 69357

CLASSIC ELITE YARNS
300A Jackson Street
Lowell, MA 01852

CLECKHEATON
distributed by
Plymouth Yarns

COLORADO YARNS
PO Box 217
Colorado Springs, CO 80903

DALE OF NORWAY
N16 W23390 Stoneridge
Drive, Suite A
Waukesha, WI 53188

GGH
distributed by
Muench Yarns

GARNSTUDIO
distributed by
Aurora Yarns

JCA
35 Scales Lane
Townsend, MA 01469

JO SHARP
distributed by
KFI

KIC2, LLC
2220 Eastman Ave. #105
Ventura, CA 93003

KFI
35 Debevoise Ave.
Roosevelt, NY 11575

KARABELLA YARNS
1201 Broadway
New York, NY 10001

KOIGU WOOL DESIGNS
RR#1
Williamsford, ON N0H 2V0

MUENCH YARNS
285 Bel Marin Keys Blvd.
Unit J
Novato, CA 94949-5724

NORO YARNS
distributed by
KFI

PATON YARNS
PO Box 40
Listowel, ON N4W3H3

PLYMOUTH YARN
PO Box 28
Bristol, PA 19007

REYNOLDS
distributed by
JCA

SCHOOLHOUSE PRESS
6899 Cary Bluff
Pittsville, WI 54466

SKACEL COLLECTION, INC.
PO Box 88110
Seattle, WA 98138-2110

TAHKI YARNS
distributed by
Tahki•Stacy Charles, Inc.

TAHKI•STACY CHARLES, INC.
8000 Cooper Ave.
Brooklyn, NY 11222

CANADIAN RESOURCES

Write to US resources for mail-order availability of yarns not listed.

AURORA YARNS.
PO Box 28553
Aurora, ON L4G 6S6

CLASSIC ELITE YARNS
distributed by
S. R. Kertzer, Ltd.

CLECKHEATON
distributed by
Diamond Yarn

DIAMOND YARN
9697 St. Laurent
Montreal, PQ H3L 2N1
and
155 Martin Ross, Unit #3
Toronto, ON M3J 2L9

KOIGU WOOL DESIGNS
RR#1
Williamsford, ON N0H 2V0

LES FILS MUENCH, CANADA
5640 rue Valcourt
Brossard, Quebec
J4W 1C5 Canada

PATONS ®
PO Box 40
Listowel, ON N4W 3H3

S. R. KERTZER, LTD.
105A Winges Rd.
Woodbridge, ON L4L 6C2

UK RESOURCES

Not all yarns used in this book are available in the UK. For yarns not available, make a comparable substitute or contact the US manufacturer for purchasing and mail-order information.

SILKSTONE
12 Market Place
Cockermouth
Cumbria, CA13 9NQ
Tel: 01900-821052

THOMAS RAMSDEN GROUP
Netherfield Road
Guiseley
West Yorks LS20 9PD
Tel: 01943-872264

VOGUE KNITTING CAPS & HATS TWO

Editor-in-Chief
TRISHA MALCOLM

Art Director
CHI LING MOY

Executive Editor
CARLA S. SCOTT

Instructions Editor
MARI LYNN PATRICK

Patterns Editor
KAREN GREENWALD

Knitting Editor
JEAN GUIRGUIS

Yarn Editor
VERONICA MANNO

Editorial Coordinator
MICHELLE LO

Photography
EYE[4]MEDIA

Book Manager
THERESA MCKEON
CARA BECKERICH

Production Manager
DAVID JOINNIDES

■

President, Sixth&Spring Books
ART JOINNIDES

LOOK FOR THESE OTHER TITLES IN THE *VOGUE KNITTING ON THE GO!* SERIES...

■

BABY BLANKETS
BABY GIFTS
BABY KNITS
BAGS & BACKPACKS
CAPS & HATS
CHUNKY KNITS
KIDS KNITS
MITTENS & GLOVES
PILLOWS
SCARVES
SOCKS
SOCKS TWO
TEEN KNITS
TODDLER KNITS
VESTS
VINTAGE KNITS
WEEKEND KNITS